ISBN: 1450542662
ISBN-13: 9781450542661

To
My Wife
MARJORIE

PREFACE

And HAFIZ has also left the shrine
I bet he's coming to have some wine

Hafiz was born as Shamsuddin Mohamed in 1320 AD, in Shiraz, Persia, the modern Iran. He lost his father when relatively young and had to do unskilled work as a child to help support his family. He memorized the Quran at an early age and was, therefore, called Hafiz, a title he later adopted as his pen name. He taught himself and became a scholar, a mystic, and a poet par excellence. He also became a favorite of kings, princes, and ministers, and spent the rest of his life in relative affluence. He married and had at least one son, but his wife and son died in his lifetime. He died in 1381 AD at the age of 61 years in Shiraz, and was buried there.

Though HAFIZ is poor and odd and flawed
He has the treasure of the love of God

Undoubtedly, Hafiz is one of the greatest poets this world has seen. Much of his poetry has been lost over the centuries. Only about six hundred poems, mainly odes, have survived, and these are revered by very, very many. He has been translated in many, many languages, including English, many, many times.

Translation, by its very nature, cannot capture the taste and flavor of the original, and this is especially true of the translations of Hafiz. It is impossible to translate the music, the beat, the rhythm, and the flow of his poetry, but I tried to retain some of the flavor by translating his odes, couplet by couplet

The heavens are empty, and the world is naught
It's an illusion, in which we are caught

Hafiz is a lover with a capital L. He loves music, dance, wine, and women, and indeed all the good things in life, but above all, he is a lover of love and beauty. He coins exquisite words and phrases and combines them to produce exceedingly beautiful musical sounds. See, how he paints the picture of feminine beauty:

By the magical eyes of my beautiful doll
By her graceful figure, so slim, so tall

By the fountain of life that is in her lips
By her narrow waist and her swinging hips

By her lovely face that looks like a rose
By her glowing cheeks and her precious nose

By her silken tresses and her golden curls
By her voluptuous mouth which is full of pearls

By her playful eyes and the way she winks
By the wine red and the way she drinks

By her charming manners, her elegance, and grace
By her stately carriage, her poise, and her pace

For her pity and kindness does HAFIZ crave
He remains her humble and a lowly slave

And look, how he describes the pleasure of drinking in the garden surrounded by the beauty of nature:

I went to the garden and drank some ale
And heard the wailing of the nightingale

Blooming there also was a beautiful rose
But, unlike the birds, it had no woes

It looked so happy, so vigorous, so proud
Standing alone and above the crowd

The narcissus also was looking very grand
Had a tulip in waiting with a cup in hand

The iris there also was lashing its tongue
Scolding them all, whether old or young

And holding a flask was there a lass
Pouring red wine in everyone's glass

And there was HAFIZ singing his song
Telling us to come and sing along

He does not distinguish appearance from reality, human from divine, and neither can we when we read him. In human beauty he sees the glory and majesty of God. For him, the bar is a place of worship, the bar keeper a teacher, and the wine the spirit of Divine knowledge. And the barmaid, yes the barmaid, is a houri straight from paradise, so beautiful, so obliging. See how he portrays her:

The maid of the bar, she is truly divine
Just see how she wets her lips with wine

If you don't kiss it, it would be a sin
For nothing is sweeter than her dimpled chin

Just see how she serves and how she smiles
Our faith and reason, oh, how she beguiles

And look at her body and her narrow waist
For whoever made her had a wonderful taste

But above all else, he is a mystic and a man of God. When he looks for God, he finds Him everywhere, and most surprisingly, within his own heart:

My heart was looking for the magic bowl
When it was there, built in his soul

O mystic look in my clear wine
In it you'll see the image divine

I see in the tavern the glory of God
But everyone thinks it's all very odd

He may be hidden but He is also bare
You also can see him, if you only care

Whether on earth or up in the sky
He never is hidden from His lover's eye

And though HAFIZ is poor and odd, and flawed
He has in his heart the love of God

And at the end of his mystical journey when he faces God he says:

> *The realm of nothingness did I finally reach*
> *And the limits of being, I managed to breach*
>
> *Open not the mouth, and blink not the eye*
> *For allowed you aren't to speak or pry*
>
> *There's nothing to ask, and none to inform*
> *No life, no body, no shape, no form*

But nothing captures Hafiz more in his totality than the following ode:

> *With the bar all swept, and nice and clean*
> *The keeper of the bar was doing the routine*
>
> *The topers were kneeling to show their respect*
> *Although they're always so proud and erect*
>
> *The shine of the wine was shaming the moon*
> *And the maids were gracing the happy saloon*
>
> *The angels from Heaven were also there*
> *And the lovely houris were dancing everywhere*
>
> *The beauties while drinking couldn't stay quiet*
> *They were tempting and flirting and causing a riot*
>
> *Then the lady luck also came down there*
> *With all her glory, and pomp, and flair*
>
> *I also went down just to say hello*
> *To the keeper who said, "My good fellow*
>
> *"You're coming from the shrine, a fine place*
> *Looking in the tavern the Divine grace*
>
> *"But never will you reach your worthy goal*
> *Unless you've awakened your sleeping soul*
>
> *"But if you can perform this daring feat*
> *The moon will bow and kiss your feet*

4

"And your reason, with all its pomp and pride
To be your slave it'll surely decide

"And our HAFIZ says if you stay in the pub
You'll become a member of a blessed club"

Khalid Hameed Shaida, MD
E. Mail. khalmeed@aol.com
Web: www.writing.com/authors/khalmeed

1
Ila ya ayyohas saaqi ader kaasan wa naawilha

Come, fill the cup and ease my pain
This pain is driving me insane

The scent of her hair is beyond compare
And tangled am I in her curly hair

Love mystic knows, be it divine
Endure he cannot without the wine

So go with the flow, and do your best
For on your way there is no rest

Storms there are awful to face
Of which on shore there is no trace

And do evil not for it will show
And God and man will come to know

And a mystic, Hafiz, is bound to be fake
If pleasures of life he doesn't forsake

2

Aey faroagh e maah e husn az roo e rakhshaan e shuma

Your face is reflected in the beauty of moon
So when you're away, the moon is in ruin

My love, I'm dying to see your face
So whether I live, depends on your grace

Oh, how I remember your curly hair
Covering your face when flying in the air

Your eyes so full of magic and charm
Enchanting us all, but causing no harm

Your face with radiance, charm, and glow
It makes life happy and fortunes grow

The scent that surrounds your body entire
Envies the incense, but the roses admire

When I think of it, my heart does leap
I feel so happy, I can't go to sleep

When during the night to the bar I go
The ladies of night, they all tell me – no!

It seems that people who live in this town
Are not very kind, for always they frown

But there is our king who is honest and fair
Whose virtue and justice I praise everywhere

So daring, so valiant, so mighty, so high
That him do we worship; for him do we die

His kingdom so big, and his castle so high
That slave unto him is the mighty sky

And now with HAFIZ let's go and pray
May your lips get sweeter day after day

3

Ager aan turk e sheeraazi ba dast aarad dil e ma ra

O Turko girl, you come to me and in my arms retire
And I'll give your beauty spot ol' Tamerlane's empire

Oh, come to me and fill the cup and leave the razz-ma-tazz
For find you will in Heaven too no garden of Shiraz

Look, as soon as they come in town, the beauties there and then
Like Golden Horde, they plunder all the hearts and souls of men

Those lovely girls are proud and rude and full of subterfuge
And need these dolls for lips and cheeks no lipstick and no rouge

The day I saw your lovely face, my heart, my soul, my life!
Yes, instantly I understood the case of Potiphar's wife

Come, drink and dance and be merry; enjoy your every breath
For solve he can't, the wise man, the puzzle of life and death

Look, young you are, and strong, and well, but there's a lot to know
So reject you not the counsel of an old and wise pro

But worry you not that the bitter words aren't so proper and hip
Like gems and pearls, they drop from your that lovely ruby lip

And listen to HAFIZ his verses are the strings of gems and pearls
And even the sky, on hearing him, its starry garland hurls

4

Ba mulaazimaan e sultaan keh rasaanad ein dua ra

To the palace guard can someone go and very humbly say
That the needy ones who come to you, O turn them not away

A stony heart in a bosom soft, and a fair and lovely face
Uncommon it is a conjunction and very rare a case

My rivals are a crafty lot, my foes so vile and vicious
So help, O Lord, a hapless me, for You are so kind and gracious

When rouge you put on your rosy cheek, on fire you set my heart
But when I put my lips on it, O why do you act so tart?

When on your eyes, those shiny blue, you put a little mascara
With just a look you instantly do kill me, O my Farah

I wait and wait all night long, but come you don't, my dear
And when I ask the reason why, a lame excuse I hear

When you're gone, my lonely heart O how it aches and aches
And when you don't come back to me, it cracks, it rends, it breaks

And when someday you braid your hair and make a lovely chain
On seeing it, my crazy heart goes only more insane

The magic in those eyes of yours, oh, how it rends my heart
And the charming look from you, my love, does hit me like a dart

And when I say I love your lips, do not you please disdain
For what I need is a tiny kiss to cure me of my pain

And if you send, with the morning breeze, the scent of your curly hair
I'll be cured of all my ills, inhaling the fragrant air

And if you bring the ruby wine and give him a sip of it
Pray for you your HAFIZ will, and never complain a bit

5

Taa kay ba dard e hijr kuni naatawaan mara

How long, how long your absence and pain
It makes no sense; it's so insane?

Tormenting, I know, you love so much
How long this agony will you maintain?

I have no one but you, my love
How can then I from love refrain?

How can a life without you I live
When a moment of sleep I can't obtain?

Surrounded am I with pain and sorrow
To whom, my dear, do I complain?

It was so nice you came for a while
But now I am back to crying again

And HAFIZ says I am going to die
I can't survive this emotional drain

6

Doosh az masjid soo e maikhaana aamad peer e ma

Look, O mystic, the master is at the tavern's door tonight
So we should also follow him, for it should be all right

And when he sees us with cups in hand, he'll surely give us a nod
Because it is our destiny, and it's the will of God

With the master himself getting high, enjoying a merry song
Who then, O mystic friends, can say that we are in the wrong?

When the wise see our ecstasy in the chains of braided hair
They would also like to be in a lovely, curly snare

And the holy men, when they find us necking and kissing the lips
O they will never use their whips, and from us will take their tips

The stony hearts will melt away and lose their ugly tiff
And all our sighs, and moans, and groans will pay off in a jiff

And happy so we all will be in the bonds of curly hair
That when the curls do fly in the air, our bonds will never tear

And cover the moon, like clouds they, when the curls do fly apart
The darkness will be the source of light and delight the lonely heart

And even though our sighs are like arrows flying all over
They hit no one; they hurt no one; they only like to hover

Be not surprised, O mystic friends, to see him in the fore
When HAFIZ sees the master too is at the tavern's door

7

Saaqi ba noor e baada berafrooz jaam e ma

Come, light up the cup with sparkling wine
For life is lovely, and everything is fine

In the wine reflected when I see your face
I feel exalted by the Divine Grace

Like cypress tree, when you swing and sway
The beauties you throw in disarray

The one who loves can never die
For love is eternal, no one can deny

From love, when drunk, you do not shrink
So happy are those with whom you drink

Don't listen to the preacher who talks of sin
On the Judgment Day, our wine will win

O breeze of spring, to my darling tell
You touch her often; you know her well

"I still remember the day we met
Though you've forgotten, I cannot forget

"My fate it was, and I bore the cost
Regret I not having loved and lost

"If you don't believe, and think I am a sham
Come talk to my patron, the generous Quam

"And think of your HAFIZ, and don't say no
Come back to him, for he loves you so"

8

Saaqi bagzaar az kuff e khud ratl e garaan ra

Come, my love, and fill the cup, and fill it to the brim
So life becomes more livable and not so dim and grim

And listen you not to the holy man; he is always finding fault
But expect you what from a petty man, worth who is not his salt?

For knows he not, when you look for God, you find him everywhere
Be it the temple, mosque, or pub, or be it here or there

And the wise men, the wine of love, they never, ever touch
They think they know what's there to know; in fact they know not much

Though a learned man is HAFIZ not, he does know what he wants
He takes his women, and wine, and whatever else God grants

9

Saaqia barkhaiz o dardeh jaam ra

O Come, my love, and fill the cup, for it's for me a must
And let's bury my sorrow and pain forever in the dust

With ruby wine in my hand, I'll be the talk of the town
And there will be no need for me to wear my mystic's gown

Though people say that a wise man should try to make a name
But I am not a wise man; I've nothing to do with fame

The ethics of sensuality let us all bury in the dust
For we are not for casual love; we have no use for lust

Burning we are in the flame of love; our hearts are full of fire
So let us hope that the fire in us will someday others inspire

And let's be proud of what we are; love as much as we want
Let people say whatever they want; we are above their cant

Believe it or not but true it is, we've lost our ease and rest
For the love of one, who is famous for her most comforting breast

To anyone who has seen my girl, so tall, so slim, so trim
In the park, the pines and conifers will look so very dim

So cheer you up, and the happiness do not you ever shun
And eat, and drink, and be merry; have lots and lots of fun

And be patient, O HAFIZ dear, and don't torment your soul
For one day she will come to you, and you will reach your goal

10
Soofi bia keh aaina saaf ast jaam ra

O mystic, look in my clear wine
In it you'll see the image Divine

The lovers all know the mystery of being
Which the learned can't, without them seeing

For seeing the truth, one needs a vision
So chase not pray an empty illusion

And learn to love, for love is divine
Its limits and bounds you can't define

And pray to the Lord for mercy and grace
And hope someday you'll see His face

Better be happy with what you get
And for the rest, oh, do not fret

And when in a pub, take a drink or two
For more than that is not for you

And having lost the fancy of youth
In the ripe old age, you seek the truth

So, HAFIZ, seek to the maximum
For you're a follower of Solomon and Jum

11
Salaah e kaar kuja o mun e kharaab kuja

Between proud and pious, and a humble sinner
It is hard to say who'll be the winner

For one is a lover, and the other is holy
And one is stern; the other is jolly

I want no mosque, no mystic's gown
Give me some wine for my sorrow to drown

Your company is all for which I hunger
I crave your mercy; I love your anger

My rival does not see your charm
His feelings are cold; his heart not warm

But my heart is crazy, pure and simple!
It loves your cheek, your mole, your dimple

Without you, darling, it misses a beat
And if you'd allow, it'll live in your street

Ask HAFIZ, if me you do not believe
For a lover like me there is no reprieve

12
Saba ba lutf bagoo aan ghizaal e raana ra

O breeze, you go to my little doe, and very humbly say
"Looking for you in the wilderness, I have totally lost my way

"O beauty queen of the universe, O fairest of the fair
What happens to me, the hapless one, you have to also care

"O sugary one, your juicy lips with the vintage ruby wine
Resist I can't the urge to kiss; to me they are divine

"O you're like a budding flower, so young, so full of pride
Like nightingale, I sing to you; me don't you please deride

"And all you need is kindness and a lock of curly hair
To catch a really wise one, you do not need a snare

"And when you sit with your chosen one and drink in the moonlit night
Do think of me who loves you so, and who isn't so very bright"

But those who like them tall and fair, with beautiful brown eyes
They should expect no loyalty from them if they are wise

If there is a flaw in a perfect beauty, it's not conceit or pride
Fidelity is what she sadly lacks; it cannot be denied

A loser you are in love, HAFIZ, but your verses have a ring
On hearing them, does Jupiter dance and Venus begins to sing

13

Hangaam e naubahaar gul az boostaan juda

Oh, pluck not a flower from the garden in spring
Just think of the sorrow such parting will bring

The trees in grief, their leaves will shed
The birds will weep and refuse to sing

And taking the flowers to the florist's shop
Is like the death doing its thing

It's like a groom dying in the wedding
And the anxious bride not getting her ring

Look, so many beauties are sleeping in dust
And under your feet is a mighty king

So tread you gently, when you walk on ground
Lest hurt you those who've lost everything

And forget not, HAFIZ, when you go to God
What here you forsake, there you'll bring

14
Aafaab az roo e o shud dar hijaab

O hides the sun from my brilliant moon
Like the shadow does from the sun at noon

My heartless moon, when she drops her veil
The stars and planets look dim and pale

And I am so awed by her beauty and grace
That her in my dream, I'm afraid to embrace

Oh, what a lovely beauty and her ugly veil
And what a hapless lover and his dreadful wail

So when I drink the ruby wine
I drink not wine but the tears of mine

But there is no liquor in this dreadful city
They say it's forbidden; oh, what a pity

If only he could see a heart on fire
The censor will soften and surely retire

For the fire of love, after years and years
You can't put out by shedding tears

And don't say, HAFIZ, that love is bad
It's simply divine, but yes, it's sad

15

Zay baagh e wasl e to yaabad riyaaz e Rizwaan aab

Your presence makes Eden a true paradise
And in your absence, it's a devil's device

From the fountain of Heaven has come your youth
In your magical eyes, there is the ultimate truth

Your cheeks make roses of Heaven look silly
You're slimmer and taller than the Forbidden Tree

Your beauty is reflected in the youth of spring
And the praise of your grace the birds all sing

All nectar comes from your lips and mouth
Without them, surely, there will be a drought

If only you'll give me a little attention
Between you and me, there'll be no tension

And if you think I'm a greedy fool
Just look, for you how the pious drool

Oh, how I love your luscious red lips
From which the honey constantly drips

But HAFIZ tells me it's idle talk
And the door won't open until I knock

16

Subh e doulat meedamad koo jaam humchoo aaftaab

The glorious morning is here again; the sun is finally up
Come, O my love, and bring the jug, and fill my morning cup

Come, bring your harp, and sit by me, and play a happy tune
Let's enjoy our lovely youth; let's eat, and drink, and croon

And let us hold each other's hands; let's hop, and turn, and dance
And let's not waste the happy days, and let's not lose this chance

It seems to me that you and me, we make a lovely team
Which makes me wonder, is it true, or is it just a dream?

Oh, when I see your cheeks and lips, I think they are divine
It seems the one, who made them so, drank lots of rosy wine

And putting together your charming eyes with magical, mystic gaze
It is a feat that must require not six but sixty days

It cannot be an accident; it is surely by design
The union of my golden cup with the vintage ruby wine

And Hafiz has a store of words, that his verses when she hears
Picks Venus all these gems and pearls, and puts them around her ears

17

Aan siyehchirdeh keh sheereeni e aalam baa oost

She is darkest, and loveliest, and sweetest of all
So charming, so happy, so fair, and so tall

Her mouth is sweet, and her lips are red
She has magic in eyes, and wisdom in head

A model of virtue, with an angel's face
Paradigm of beauty, elegance, and grace

On her golden face, a mole so cute
As tempting and luring as the Forbidden Fruit

When pert and saucy, she wounds the heart
Then practice she does, her healing art

With her stony heart, she can kill and heist
And amazingly, also, she has the breath of Christ

And tells me HAFIZ I shouldn't be distressed
For being her lover, I'm truly blessed

18

Aan paik e naamwar keh raseed az dayaar e dost

Bless you, O courier, my greetings to you
An amulet for me is her message new

Splendor it shows, and her grandeur anew
An honor and trust that belong to few

I have surrendered for her my all
But a sacrifice this I wouldn't call

Her beauty rules the earth and the sky
And all in there, whether low or high

A queen she is; unique is her throne
She stands above, and she stands alone

And though she is beyond my reach
I wait and wait, and beg and beseech

When passes she by, she never says hi
Though dirt of her feet, I rub in my eye

I sit at her gate in the hope someday
"Hello! My dear," she will stop and say

There's nothing like love, whatever the cost
And her HAFIZ is proud, though he has loved and lost

19
Agarcheh baada farahbakhsh o baad gulbaiz ast

Though air is fragrant and the wine delicious
It's now forbidden, and the censor is vicious

And when she comes with a flask of wine
You can be sure it's a good sign

But hide, O mystic, the cup in your gown
The liquor is forbidden by order of crown

The stain of wine you wash with tears
And do it quietly, lest someone hears

And expect not luck from the horrible fate
Be merry today; for tomorrow not wait

This fate is destructive; it does its thing
Distinguish it doesn't a beggar from king

Early in the morning, you wake up and pray
And God will grant you whatever you say

And a lot, O HAFIZ, your verses are worth
You've become famous around the earth

20
Aey naseem e sahar aaraamgeh e yaar kujaast

O morning breeze, you tell me please where is my girl's abode?
The pretty one, and the charming one, with a lovely graceful mode

Drifted have I in wilderness, in order to see her face
I've even seen the Burning Bush, but her I could not trace

And all of us, who abide the earth, are imperfect at best
So do not think that the people in pub are not like the rest

Blessed is one who reads a book but reads it between the print
Not the rest of us who see the clues, but never take a hint

And happy is one who loves and loves and does not ever despair
But a wise man, who knows not love, he does not really care

So come to me, and be with me, and put out the flaming fire
The fire of love that is consuming my body and soul entire

And though I have whatever I want and whatever I do desire
But in your absence, I am sick and tired, and my condition is dire

With you not there, I have lost my all, my soul, my faith, my reason
And crying and crying, all day, all night, I have lost my eyes, my vision

I cannot bear the sight of sheik; he does no one inspire
He says I love an infidel, something I don't admire

So let me find my rest and peace in the shade of your curly hair
I do not care for the freedom here; I'd rather be a captive there

And HAFIZ says I shouldn't despair; the winter is part of life
And to have a rose without a thorn is life without strife

27

21

Imrooz shaah e anjuman e dilbaraan yakiest

Oh, she is the queen of beauty, so fair, so bright, so sunny
And she's my one and only; oh, she is my honey bunny

And to her I must surrender my life, my faith, my reason
She's all I have, O preacher, and this is beyond revision

And when you are a lover, you give, and give, and give
You do not think of profit, and that's the way you live

In the thinking of a lover, there are no twists, no kinks
He always does whatever he says; he says whatever he thinks

And whatever she asks, O HAFIZ dear, you give, you do, you render
You cannot be a lover if your will you don't surrender

22

Bia keh qasr e amal sakht sust bunyaad ast

Desire is a castle built in the air
A heartbreak house, a place of despair

O preacher, you think, it cannot be
But a captive of love is truly free

Listen to the old when they give advice
To ignore their counsel is not very nice

Don't be allured by the worldly pleasure
This world is unfaithful, by any measure

One night in the bar, when I was drunk
An angel came and said, "You punk!

"What are you doing, in this dusty place?
You are an eagle, it's a disgrace

"Everyone in Heaven, is looking for you
What are you doing, trapped in this zoo?

"But don't you worry, and don't despair
Listen to the mystic, for he's aware

"You have no choice; listen, you clod!
Surrender your will to the will of God

"Look, in this garden, time goes fast
The smiling flowers of spring don't last"

In verse, O HAFIZ, you have the throne
You stand above, and you stand alone

23

Banaal bulbul agar baa munat sar e yaariest

O singing bird, you're my kind of guy
We are lovers both, and we can only cry

Wherever the air does her tresses kiss
There is no need for the ambergris

Come, fill the cup, and let me get drunk
My arrogance and pride have made me a skunk

So let us drink and not be so dense
The spring is no time for penitence

You can meet your love, though it'll be fake
Dreaming is better than being awake

The snare of her hair is not for the straight
Only a devious lover does bite the bait

There's more to love than passion and sighs
The beauty is more than the charming eyes

It is just not lips that we lovers admire
There're many more things that ignite desire

To be her slave is no ordinary thing
I'd rather be her vassal than be a king

Money sans talent is nothing to admire
No mystic would want the kingly attire

It hurts us, HAFIZ, whenever you cry
And hurting others, one should not try

24

Baroo ba kaar e khud aye waaiz ein cheh feryaad ast

Leave me, O preacher, and let it all be
The problem is mine, so leave it to me

The cure of my pain is there in her lips
The counsel of yours is no good to me

From naught to naught, it has come to be
Her waist is so narrow, no one can see

A slave of her beauty cares not for Eden
Her captive of love is truly free

My life is empty without her grace
Wherever I look, there always is she

If cruel she is, cry not, O heart
Surrender your will; it's God's decree

Don't be deceived; this world is a witch
She is a siren of the deep blue sea

Scorn not, O preacher, our drunken ways
It's the will of God, beyond you and me

And don't give us, HAFIZ, your wild talk
Your stories drive us all up the tree

25

Bai mehr e rukhat rooz e mara noor na maandaast

With your sunshine gone, day looks like a night
And night looks darker, which gives me a fright

Ever since you left, I've cried and cried
So much so that I've lost my sight

Even if you came, it is no use now
From body my life is taking its flight

So dark it is that the image stored
Of you in my eye is not in sight

I'm so far from you that contain they can't
My awful rivals, their sheer delight

Your absence, though it's due to my fate
I am very, very angry and very uptight

When you were here, my death was at bay
But the outlook now is not very bright

They say that patience is my only hope
But patience in me is less than slight

Although no water is left in my eyes
There's plenty of blood, both red and bright

So cry not, says HAFIZ; resign to fate
It's all written there in black and white

26
Juz aastaan e to am dar jahaan panaahay neest

In you, my love, is my only refuge
Only you can save me from deluge

Exposed, I am, to my rival's dart
My body is weak, and frail is my heart

My day and night, I spend in the bar
My only friend is the wine jar

And I don't care what happens to me
I'm between the devil and deep blue sea

But I am a slave of your charming eyes
Although I know it is not very wise

Be kind to all, whether stranger or kin
To hurt someone is a terrible sin

O beauty queen, don't be so proud
We all need you, the entire crowd

The evil and malice are all over city
Nobody has heard of mercy and pity

The traps are there, and their number huge
In you, my love, is my only refuge

Be careful, says HAFIZ, of her locks and mole
The blacks are lovely, but they take their toll

27

Haasil e kaargeh e kon o makaan ein hama neest

The heavens are empty, and the world is naught
It's an illusion in which we are caught

Her company I cherish with all my soul
The pain of her absence is beyond control

In heaven and earth, unique is she
And like my cypress, no cypress can be

O preacher, rewards of the afterlife
They aren't worth the pain and strife

So let's be happy with what we get
And about the strife, let's not fret

We are at the precipice of the void at best
In the time we have, let's drink with zest

O preacher, be proud not so of your creed
The pub isn't far from the mosque, indeed

With grief and pain, my heart is in shock
So weak it is, it can't even talk

So worry you not; make the best of it
Your pain is bound to one day remit

And though, HAFIZ, I am both famous and rich
I can kick it all without a hitch

28

Khushtar zay aish e sohbat o baagh o bahaar cheest

How pretty is the garden; how nice the spring
So come, my love, some wine you bring

And without wine and women in the paradise
There'll be nothing, O preacher, to advertise

So let's be happy, and have no strife
For after this life there may be no life

I love the chain of her braided hair
And the pangs of bondage I love to bear

The mystery of being only topers know
And the pious men only put up a show

The mystics and topers indeed are one
For the choice, being lovers, they have none

This world of ours is full of conceit
And wherever you look, there is deceit

Now the preacher is pious, and Hafiz a sinner
Let's see in Heaven who'll be the winner?

29
Dil saraparda e mohabbat e oost

My heart is a place for her to repose
So wherever she is, it stays very close

With his love for her even the mightiest king
To her two little feet does he want to cling

A beggar, a lover, a preacher, a king
According to his measure does everything

If Romeo is dead, the lovers are not
And love from their hearts you cannot blot

Oh, God may be hidden, but He is also bare
You also can see Him, if you only care

The treasure of love and the kingdom of bliss
Given us He has, whether that or this

And whether we live or whether we die
Destruction and death He'll always defy

And whether on earth or up in the sky
He never is hidden from His lover's eye

O there is no doubt that I am a sinner
But having His grace, I can be a winner

And every new flower that graces the spring
It has been ordered by the Heavenly king

And though HAFIZ is poor, and odd, and flawed
He has in his heart the love of God

36

30

Deedi keh yaar juz ser e joer o sitam nadaasht

With a stony heart and the cruel eyes
Oh, how her lovers she crucifies

She has no pity for the wounded heart
It cries and cries until it dies

And when I protest, the penance I get
By blaming it on fate she justifies

Notorious so have I now become
Not even a drunkard on me relies

So much respect have I lost that to me
A drink on credit the barman denies

A mystic who pays not homage to her
For going to Mecca he not qualifies

And blessed is lover who suffers and suffers
And the comforts of life to himself denies

And the way you say it, your rival, O HAFIZ
Can't possibly say, although he tries

31

Roosa e khuld e bareen khilwat e durwaishaanast

Retreat of the mystics is a heavenly haunt
To be in their service who wouldn't want?

Their site of worship is a place of wonder
Where day and night miracles they render

Embark when they do on the mystical way
Heaven is something they see every day

Close to the mystics, you've Midas' touch
Becomes it gold whatever you clutch

The sun and the moon come down to earth
To worship the mystics at the time of birth

The wealth of mystics is beyond compare
It is not something that one can pare

And even a king, almighty and brave
He bows to them and becomes their slave

In the world of ours, all beauty and grace
Reflections they are of a mystic's face

The high, the mighty, the giants, the kings
They gain their stature, under mystics' wings

When sees Croesus the mystics' wealth
Out of shame, he resorts to stealth

A slave am I to the grand vizier
With a mystic's nature, he has no peer

And if you're looking for the spring of youth
Find it you will in the mystic's booth

If tyranny and evil spring from the palace
In the shack of a mystic, there is no malice

O HAFIZ, be courteous in the mystics' abode
Even a king comes there in a beggar's mode

32
Roozgaareest keh soda e butaan deen e mun ast

The love of beauties has become my creed
And having the pangs is a joy indeed

Crying in her absence, I've become blind
And her without sight, I cannot find

But it has also made me fluent and witty
And famous I am throughout the city

The wine of love is a wonderful brew
For it has made me a mystic too

So rich has become my poor little heart
Tell it you can't from a king apart

Killing her lovers is her favorite sport
The dark little girl we all love to court

When she is not there, I cry and cry
My tears keep falling like stars from sky

When in her street, I seek my abode
Like flowers become the thistles on road

For the world of ours, it is a boon
My tears like stars, her face like moon

O praise not, HAFIZ, the mighty kings
You come and admire the beautiful things

33
Roo e to kas nadeed o hazaarat raqeeb hast

A darling unseen, with lovers in herds
A budding flower, with scores of birds

Not only am I, who is so poor
Lovers has God, both cultured and boor

I have a feeling, it may be bizarre
My union with Him is not very far

A temple, a mosque, pagoda, or church
Him you'll find wherever you search

An organ, a bell, a song, or a gong
In the business of worship, they all belong

The love of God is an ailment severe
There are no patients though Doctor is there

Your way of crying, O HAFIZ of mine
It rends my heart, but it's so divine

41

34

Riwaaq e manzar e chashm e mun aashiaana e tust

Oh, make my eyes your only home
In my park of love do come and roam

Your beauty spot has stolen the heart
Of a mystic like me from the very start

You are the rose, I nightingale
To sing to you, I'll never fail

The nature of ailment may be obscure
But in your lips, you have my cure

Though in your service I couldn't enroll
In the dust of your feet are my heart and soul

Of making a promise you aren't shy
But no one lies the way you lie

Oh, how I love you, I wish you knew
My heart belongs to none but you

But I'm not the only for you who craves
The stars and the moon are all your slaves

And your HAFIZ whenever his verses recites
The angels and houris he greatly delights

35

Raseeda am ba muqaamay keh laamakaan aanjaast

The realm of nothingness did I finally reach
And the limits of being I managed to breach

Open not the mouth, and blink not the eye
For allowed you aren't to speak or pry

There's nothing to ask, and none to inform
No life, no body, no shape, no form

O nightingale, go there to sing
Where neither is autumn nor the spring

And where there're no heaves, no sighs
No Juliet betrayed, no Romeo cries

And after his union, no matter how odd
No mystic's allowed to say he is God

Go there not, HAFIZ, and make no mistake
Even at night, her guardian's awake

36

Zaahid e zaahirparast az haal e ma aagaah neest

The preacher, he knows not me at all
Blame him you cannot, his mind is small

Though a mystic has hurdles many to cross
By the grace of God, he isn't at loss

The game of life is a game of chess
For a clod like me it is simply a mess

What sort of justice is it and why
I'm not allowed even to sigh?

And what is real, and what is not?
No one, we know, knows what is what

The final reality is only God
His august realm no one can trod

The wine of love is for the sincere
Of pangs and pains, they have no fear

O I am the slave of the abbot of pub
Me the preachers always wrongly rub

Of sin and virtue, they keep an account
But redemption and mercy they tend to discount

And they are so lost in the nitty and gritty
Unable are they to see God's pity

If HAFIZ is honored, it is for his vision
Of money and power, he has no provision

37

Zay girya mardum e chashmam nashista dar khoonast

Your lovers are pouring their blood in tears
Their lives are full of pangs and fears

And think when I do of your lips and eyes
I drink my blood in wine's disguise

If only I could get a glimpse of you
The joys of life I could renew

Your lips and eyes do me entice
Your snare of hair is my paradise

Graceful you are, like a cypress tree
Your words are sweet as sweet can be

Come, fill the cup, and soothe my pain
My peace of mind O let me regain

Your absence, my love, I cannot bear
Tears I shed of blood in despair

Maybe someday, I'll again be glad
But as of now, my life is sad

But come, says HAFIZ, don't be a loon
Crying for her is crying for the moon

38

Zaan yaar e dilnawaazam shukreest baa shikaayat

To her I'm grateful, but then I'm not
She once made a promise, and then she forgot

Oh, how much I served her without reward
How thankless a mistress she is, O Lord

Not a drop of wine to a thirsty toper
No love, no mercy, no pity for a pauper

Beware, O heart, of the snare of her locks
Innocents she catches in flocks and flocks

The traps are there on the way everywhere
The journey is endless; beware, beware!

The arrow of her gaze can kill in a wink
You fall on the ground before you can blink

For my queen of beauty, my heart is on fire
With yearning, and longing, and burning desire

In the dark of night, I've gone astray
O my guiding star, do show me the way

Oh, I am dishonored; I am disgraced
To be a lover is to be debased

A lover's journey is full of agony
Wherever you look you see only misery

If her, says HAFIZ, you want to embrace
Just learn to recite the Quran with grace

46

39

Sehn e bustaan zoaqbakhsh o sohbat e yaaraan khushast

Surrounded by flowers, with a lovely friend
Drinking and dancing it does recommend

The morning breeze brings the scent
To make the heart and soul content

O nightingale, do come and sing
The spring will soon be on the wing

And God loves those who're up all night
Who seek His mercy and are contrite

The life is short, and its joys few
So the way of life of a toper pursue

One night, I heard a voice, which said
"Do not forget you'll soon be dead

"With God, O HAFIZ, try to connect
And the worldly joys you must reject"

40

Saba agar guzaray uftadat ba kishwar e dost

Go to her place, O morning air
Bring the scent of her curly hair

I'll give my life if you do confer
And bring a hopeful sign from her

Whatever you do, bring you must
From her door a handful of dust

Even in dreams, I see no sign
That in reality she'll ever be mine

Like a cypress tree, she's tall and slim
But I've no reach; my chances are dim

And values she little a lover like me
But to me she is precious as precious can be

Even her dog I must gratify
For a dog to her is dearer than I

Says HAFIZ, "Establish a little dialogue
And try to become a friend of her dog"

41

Soofi az purtoo e mai raaz e nihaani daanist

In wine, O mystic, is the secret of being
This image is real; O it's worth seeing

The flowers and colors know the singing birds
For the meaning's vital, and not the words

And love knows only the heart of man
Experience this feeling no creature can

The wine in secret I try to drink
Unknown to the censor and to his fink

And if she is callous, it's by design
Indeed her malice is very benign

Look, how she turns into pearl and gem
The dirt and stones by looking at them

With reason to fathom love is lunatic
So don't even try, for it's all magic

With pride a flower does never glow
If ravage of winter it happens to know

What makes you, HAFIZ, without a peer
Is the company you enjoy of the grand vizier

42

Subh e doulat tuloe e talaat e oost

Her glowing face makes the morning bright
Her raven hair gives darkness to night

Seeing her face, sun sets at noon
And bows to her, the crescent moon

Facing her, cypress stands not tall
Seeing her face, feels the tulip small

The scent in flowers is from her hair
And sing her praise the birds everywhere

And iris, the talker, she has a fit
Whenever she sees her grace and wit

Though poverty is very hard to bear
When you're with her, you do not care

Go not to the doctor when you're ill
Just go to her, and cure you she will

O mystic, the hurdles you've in the way
Ordained are they; they are okay

The hearts of all men she has won
O HAFIZ, I'm not the only one

43

Kunoon keh dar kaff e gul jaam e baada e saafast

With flowers holding the cups of wine
The birds are happy, and the bees are fine

Let's go to the park with a book of verse
Let the thinkers alone, and let them converse

For the ruler of the city has just announced
That dancing and drinking can't be denounced

Whatever is given, you take and keep
And drink the wine, expensive or cheap

With struggle and strife, you make a truce
Renounce the world and be a recluse

And don't you worry about friends and foes
Just say good-bye to the world of woes

And though it's true, for the sake of God
Say not, O HAFIZ, our sheik is a fraud

44

Laal e sairaab bakhoon tishna lab e yaar e mun ast

So thirsty for blood is her ruby lip
It'll take your heart and tear and rip

With lashes so long, and eyes so black
Of lovers for her there is no lack

O guide, please don't leave me here
Go farther a little; her place is near

With such a dearth of faith and trust
Lucky am I that love her I must

The smell of flowers, and the scent in the air
It is all because of her curly hair

Nothing would grow in the garden for years
If it were not for the flood of my tears

A kiss of her lips, says it I need
Her eye, my doctor, so aptly indeed

Your verses, O HAFIZ, wouldn't be so neat
If her lips and mouth weren't so sweet

45

Merhaba aey paik e mushtaaqaan badeh paeghaam e dost

Bless you, O courier; do not demur
Give me the message you brought from her

Whenever I think of her lips and eyes
My passion for them, I cannot disguise

Her locks are a snare, her mole a bait
To fall in the trap, I can hardly wait

Whoever does sip the wine of her lip
On wit and wisdom he loses the grip

Although I write her sheets and sheets
Seriously my letters she never greets

And though she knows I love her a lot
Oh, what's the use; she loves me not

So day and night, I sit in her street
Hoping to catch the dirt of her feet

But, HAFIZ, my pain I must endure
For the ailment of love there is no cure

46

Namidaanam dil e bulbul zay ishq roo e gul choon ast

When flirting with them the flower curtails
It breaks the hearts of the nightingales

The peace and patience of lovers decrease
As charm and grace of the beauties increase

With beautiful girls, so saucy and vain
No wonder the lovers go all insane

And beauties, whenever they drop their veils
Among the lovers, how madness prevails

When flowers are holding the cups of wine
Whatever you do in the garden is fine

At a time like this, when all is well
It's such a pity if you don't revel

Be happy O HAFIZ, and thank your star
The life is short; let's go to the bar

47
Al Ghayaas aey maaya e jaan al Ghayaas

The only one I have is she, O God
And look what she did to me, O God

The spring of life she has in her lips
And I am so very thirsty, O God

And in her absence, I cannot survive
But her I cannot even see, O God

Here I'm drowning in tears of blood
And hide she cannot her glee, O God

And dying I am of the wounds of her darts
Inflicted she has such injury, O God

Her glances are arrows; her lashes darts
An expert she is in archery, O God

A victim I am of my cruel fate
There's nothing but misery and agony, O God

My ailments all are because of her
And only she has the remedy, O God

My fate is brutal, callous, and vicious
And victim am I of its cruelty O God

Entangled so very, I'm in her curls
Increased it has complexity, O God

Trapped in the well of her silver chin
HAFIZ can never be free, O God

48

Baazam hawa e aan gul e raanast al Ghayaas

I am in love again, O Lord
Passion I cannot contain, O Lord

My heart that sought and found peace
Is again in constant pain, O Lord

A mystic drunk with Divine spirit
From wine he cannot abstain, O Lord

Esteemed he was, but now his fame
Acquired it has a stain, O Lord

And HAFIZ now, as the rest of lovers
Become he has insane, O Lord

49
Dard e ma ra neest darmaan al Ghayaas

Our sorrow has no cure, O God
How long can we endure, O God

The lovely ones are robbers all
Pillage and death they ensure, O God

Our life they take when a kiss they give
Oh, how we lovers they lure, O God

We must give up for them our creed
The infidels all make sure, O God

For a moment of joy of being with them
A life apart we endure, O God

We know rejection will follow soon
Whenever they make an overture, O God

Why HAFIZ is happy whenever he cries?
This whole thing is very obscure, O God

50

Aatish ander aab afsurdast ya mai dar zujaaj

Is the wine red or is it on fire
Or is it a reflection of my burning desire?

A pleasure it is for lovers to drink
For care they not what preachers think

These hapless lovers the wine consoles
It sooths their hearts and warms their souls

They come in drunk, and drunk they leave
And being not sober, they do not grieve

Come, O my love, and show your face
Let everyone see your beauty and grace

Do help those please who are in need
And needy and broke are lovers indeed

But though your lovers are poor and needy
Unlike the rich, they are not at all greedy

And in life, says HAFIZ, you play your part
And do something good, and then depart

51

Sazad keh az hama e dilbaraan sitaani baaj

No wonder the beauties pay tribute to her
Their queen she is; to her they defer

Her eyes have conquered Khata and Khutan
Her locks are the rulers of Hindustan

Her face is brighter than the sun at noon
Her curls like clouds do cover her moon

Her mouth is the source of life's spring
Her waist is as thin as a musical string

The nature of your pain is very obscure
Which if she cannot, no one can cure

So packed with sugar are her ruby lips
That from them, when she talks, the honey drips

But she can also be very, very tart
And break into pieces your dear little heart

For her, O HAFIZ, that you rave and crave
You are no more to her than a lowly slave

52

Az mun e soekhta aan yaar nameepusad heetch

Burnt up am I; cares she not
For my low and high; cares she not

She is my doctor, and patient I
I live or die; cares she not

When people see my sorry state
They wonder why cares she not?

Her absence makes me sick to death
And if I die, cares she not

Only in dreams, she's good to me
When wake up I, cares she not

Her HAFIZ is dying, O God, O God
Ask her why cares she not?

53

Aan keest kaz roo e karam baa mun wafadaari kunad

Would she be ever faithful to me
And as good to me as she can be?

Would she write when she's away
And pour me a drink and not say nay?

Oh, true it is that she can be tart
But she can also be a sweetheart

Her curly locks have a lock on me
They're pert and saucy of the first degree

Oh, how I wish she'd be my friend
Though beggars and queens do not blend

Her braided hair is like a chain
When bound by it, you do not complain

I wish the preacher, so proper and prim
Would have a drink and not look so grim

Luckily for me, when things are bad
Rescues me always my patron Samad

But HAFIZ, beware of her charming eyes
Bewitch they do and mesmerize

54

Aanaan keh khaak ra ba nazar keemia kunand

One look of His turns lead into gold
I wish me also God would behold

Unless one day He lifts His veil
His image will always be fuzzy and pale

Unseen, He causes so much uproar
What will happen if He comes to fore?

The sinners and pious are children of God
Neither preacher nor toper does He applaud

Love is the currency of kingdom of Heaven
With it you can buy not one but seven

The wine of love whoever drinks
With God Himself, he finds his links

My tale of love when tell them I
Even the stones begin to cry

For an ill like mine, there is no cure
My peace can only my death secure

Unknown to rivals if she comes to me
Oh, she will help me enormously

The beauty of Joseph whenever I see
I think of lust; I see envy

So let us drink, for the hidden sin
Is better than virtue not genuine

To win her, O HAFIZ, don't even try
For a consort of queen you don't qualify

55

Aan keh rukhsaar e tura rang e gul o nasreen daad

He, who gave her the rosy cheek
Shouldn't have made my heart so weak

Her silken tresses cruel He made
But oh, He did not come to my aid

A treasure He gave to the mighty king
And made contentment a beggar's thing

His heart when Romeo to Juliet gave
I knew this Romeo no one could save

The sensual world is a beautiful bride
But your life in dowry you must provide

And now that spring has finally come
My craving for her I can't overcome

And, HAFIZ, I am in a terrible jam
Since I've parted from Khaja Quam

56

Aan yaar kaz o khaana e ma ja e paari bood

My house enchanted the girl who made
Innocent and pure she was a maid

I left my house and went to her town
But she eloped with a handsome clown

With all my heart, I loved her because
Elegant and polished and cultured she was

To gain her favor I could not wait
But lost her I did because of my fate

About me my gal was not so keen
For I was poor, and she was a queen

A love like ours could never last
Because she came and went too fast

It's something a nightingale cannot avert
A beautiful flower must always flirt

To make it last I did what I could
And while it lasted, it was very good

Undo you cannot whatever is done
And fate, by nature, is kind to none

And a good life, HAFIZ, if you've led
It is because of the prayers you said

57

Bulbulay khoon e jigar khurd o gulay haasil kard

The bird lost all to be with the rose
But the winter came and brought the woes

And when it was singing its happy song
It suddenly heard a deadly gong

The snow was blowing, and the freeze was on
The leaves were falling, and the rose was gone

When stars in heaven it couldn't trust
My dear little moon did hide under dust

O camel driver, don't make me mad
Where is, O tell me, my Scheherazade?

Disdain them not, and do not disgrace
My tearful eyes and my dusty face

Playing with fate, I couldn't finesse
And, HAFIZ, I lost the game of chess

58

Butay daaram keh gird e gul zay sunbul saaibaan daarad

Like hyacinth is your silken hair
Covering your cheeks, so rosy and fair

May God give you immortal grace
Let the haze of time not cover your face

It's tall and slim, your cypress tree
To give it water, my tears are free

In front of all, you give me hell
And then you expect them not to tell

To everyone yes, and to me it's nay
To treat your lover, it's not the way

O you're the huntress, and I am the prey
So kill me please without delay

Your gaze is an arrow, your brow a bow
So aim the arrow, and let it go

Some wine, my love, on the ground fling
In the name of Jum, the gentle king

Save me the torment of saying good-bye
May God protect you from the evil eye

Don't fall for the rose, O nightingale
Trust it you cannot; it is so frail

To fall in love with a beautiful girl
Is like drowning looking for a pearl

They may be nameless; they may have fame
In the temple of love, they're all the same

Says HAFIZ, you can't be unkind to me
When you're as sweet as sweet can be

59

Bureed e baad e saba doesham aagaghi aawurd

The air last night brought the news
No longer will I have my cursed blues

The singer I asked to play in the bar
A melody amour on his guitar

The breeze then brought the scent of her hair
My broken heart to mend and repair

And soon an angel, from a heavenly vine
Brought for me the wine divine

This heavenly wine is a wonderful thing
It makes me dance, and sing, and swing

To HAFIZ it gives a mystical ring
And he is revered by even the king

60

Boo e khush e to her keh zay baad e saba shuneed

The fragrance brought by the morning air
A reminder it is of your curly hair

To be so friendly with a worthless toper
For the morning breeze may not be proper

O please, my queen, do listen to me
Hear my prayer; grant me the plea

Being a queen, you turn me away
And I cannot say what I want to say

I told my secret to the winter wind
It thought I was silly and only grinned

But no one wants to give me the ear
So the tale of mine I'm left to hear

To hear my tale, who would want?
I only wish I had a confidant

I use my gown to hide the wine
My abbot thinks it's just fine

My soul thrives with the smell of wine
Something the preachers always malign

My love of wine I do not hide
The abuse of preachers I take in stride

But the mysteries known to a mystics few
I was surprised that the barman knew

So listen to a mystic; he really knows
The secret of being only he can disclose

And, HAFIZ, my job is only to pray
And whatever they like, I let them say

61

Peesh az einat beesh az ein ghamkhaari e ushshaaq bood

There was a time when you were kind
Our love was the talk of the humankind

And there were nights when we would talk
Of nothing except your curly lock

And though you robbed us of our creeds
We only talked of your noble deeds

Before this world even came to be
In love with your lips and eyes were we

We also thought, from the first to last
That our love would last and outlast

And that if we were in love with you
For us some feelings you must've had too

And if my rosary broke in my hand
I was playing with your finger band

In Ramadan if we sometimes drink
It isn't wrong to be happy, we think

Though kings provide the poor with food
It's a gift of God; they shouldn't be rude

And verses of HAFIZ in paradise
Are considered precious and above any price

62

Tersam keh ashk dar gham e ma perdadar shawad

Alas, my tears my secret betrayed
My weakness for her to all displayed

So slim, and trim, and lovely is she
That within my reach she'll never be

Oh, when she comes to her balcony
Like the moon in heaven she appears to be

She's always there, in my head and heart
Her love from me unto death will part

The scent of her hair pervades my heart
With it, O breeze, I'll never part

Cry as much as you like for her
Her image, O eye, please don't blur

And in my despair, I pray and pray
Hoping that she will soften one day

O breeze, you go and tell her my woes
But in a way that no one knows

Yellow and pale I am; behold
Whatever she touches turns into gold

Moaning and groaning, to the bar I went
In the hope of easing my great torment

Be patient, O heart, though you're worn
A night is always followed by morn

My patience can turn into ruby a stone
But bleed I must, and moan, and groan

Besides the beauty that we all admire
There're other things that lovers desire

And though my rival gives her glee
Honored and trusted he'll never be

To me at my grave, if she came to greet
I'll wake up, HAFIZ, and kiss her feet

63

Tanat ba naaz e tabeebaan niyaazmand mabaad

May you never need a doctor in life
May you never be a victim of strife

Whenever you're happy, you make us glad
May you never be sorry; may you never be sad

Exposed to autumn, your flower not be
Ravage of winter may you never see

Unique is your beauty in the earth and sky
May God protect you from the evil eye

You have not only an elegant face
Your heart is pure; your soul has grace

If anyone sees you with an evil eye
May he go blind and instantly die

If an illness one has that's obscure
In verses of HAFIZ, he'll find the cure

64

Jaan bay Jamaal e jaanaan mail e jahaan nadaarad

Without her my life has no meaning
Her favoring my rival is so demeaning

Oh, on my rival she can't rely
He isn't at all an honorable guy

Of her returning, there is no sign
Whatever I do, she won't be mine

Journey of love is perilous indeed
Embark so many, but few succeed

Advice, O preacher, we do not need
Without her life is empty indeed

But do not reject the elders' advice
It's so precious and above any price

Seek contentment, and in it retire
Pain and torment come from desire

Oh, tell the flower, be proud you not;
When autumn comes, you'll decay and rot

And don't disdain the topers' way
Whatever they like let the censors say

Some people think that writing verse
Is the easiest thing in the universe

Though she is the queen of the humankind
A slave like HAFIZ she also can't find

65
Jamaalat aaftaab e her nazar baad

May your beauty delight every eye
May beauty itself you glorify

A heart not bound to your curly hair
May it be sorry; may it despair

And the deadly arrow of your charming eye
May it directly to my bosom fly

And the vintage wine of your ruby lip
May I someday leisurely sip

May my love be always renewed
And boost your beauty in magnitude

Someone who hasn't loved your face
To the humankind, he is a disgrace

May fortune smile on our noble king
May luck take him under its wing

Worships you HAFIZ, and he loves you so
May he become someday your beau

66

Chu baad azm e ser e koo e yaar khaham kard

Wherever she lives, I'll be there
So I can smell the scent of her hair

And I will put whatever have I
Under her feet when passes she by

My heart, my soul, my life, I swear
Give them I will to the scent of her hair

Without her love, I cannot live
For her there's nothing that I won't give

To the magical gaze of her charming eye
Nothing I have that I will deny

Life is lovely with women and wine
A better living no one can design

But this worldly life is not for me
A toper, O HAFIZ, I'd like to be

67

Cheh masti ast nadaanam keh roo ba ma aawurd

Her veil if she dropped, she had to be tight
Does the barman have something special tonight?

O heart, be happy and thank your star
There's something in air if she went so far

In the garden the flowers are everywhere
It's cool and pleasant, the fragrant air

The ladies of night are full of allure
The barman, in bottles, has every cure

There's frolic, and gaiety, and joy everywhere
A message from Sheba must be in the air

The night's starry, and there's full moon
And the singers are singing a happy tune

Let's go to the park with lots of wine
And sing, and dance, and drink, and dine

Your promise, O preacher, has no allure
The barmaid has all what I need and more

And HAFIZ is happy and has everything
Because he is in the court of the king

68

Khush aamad gul waz aan khushtar nabaashad

The spring has come, and the flowers are here
Let's fill our cups with wine, my dear

And sing and dance, and let's be merry
For the pleasures of life are so temporary

Let's all to the garden presently go
Lest the lovely flowers lose their glow

It's time for love, so let's not wait
Let's lose our heads and celebrate

And love is there wherever you look
It isn't something you find in a book

So listen to me and do not wait
And find a charming, beautiful mate

Of hell and heaven, O sheik, don't think
Let's go to the bar, and let's have a drink

In the tavern, my friend, there's wine galore
So let's be generous and give it to the poor

O give me the wine that drowns my sorrow
Without the headache later next morrow

My girl's so lovely, so pretty, so fair
That with her no idol can you compare

Of Sultan Avees, the mighty, the brave
I wish I could become a humble slave

So bright and shiny are the jewels of his crown
That when it sees it, the sun turns brown

If verses of HAFIZ some people deride
He simply ignores them, and takes it in stride

69

Dilbar baraft o dilshudagaan ra khabar na kard

Unknown to lovers, she left the city
Oh, in her heart she has no pity

And of my love either she knows not
Or me my luck has simply forgot

My life for her I'd like to give
But to make me suffer, she wants me to live

To soften her heart, I cry and cry
But alas, a stone I can't mollify

But the people cannot see me cry
They wipe and kiss my tearful eye

And I'm surprised that, being so precious
She loves my rival, so mean, so vicious

But me, being foolish and not very smart
I love her still with all my heart

O HAFIZ, her trust I'll never betray
You can cut my tongue if a word I say

70

Dil az mun burd o roo az mun nihaan kard

She took my heart and hid her face
It seems so very unusual a case

Though the pain of parting is killing me
Out of my heart she'll never be

Her charming eyes are cruel indeed
They wound my heart, and make it bleed

Though the night of longing is hard to survive
In the morning the breeze does come to revive

But me the one who really can cure
Pain and sorrow she makes me endure

So much sometimes do suffer I
That the harps and violins begin to cry

But how can I tell the people that she
The girl that I cherish, has done it to me

My rivals, O HAFIZ, could never do
What she did to me, and it's true

71
Dast dar halqa e aan zulf e do ta natwaan kard

With her lovely curls I'd love to play
If the price is life, I'm willing to pay

And if I could only change my fate
I wouldn't have to wait, and wait, and wait

Some headway if ever I made with her
Me my rival could never deter

I'd like to say that she looks like moon
But then she'll tell me, I am a loon

If like Venus, she decides to sing
The stars in heaven will begin to swing

Love, they say, is a mysterious thing
It conquers all and everything

So delicate a temperament does have my baby
That she thinks my litany is all very crazy

So innocent, and pure, and clean is she
With an evil eye, her no one can see

Her brow, O HAFIZ, is a perfect niche
Where the preacher can pray without a hitch

72

Doesh deedam keh malaaik dar e maikhaana zadand

Brought angels the wine to the tavern's door
Of love, to pour in the human core

Seeing wine with them, I got worked up
And begged them to pour it in my cup

And when my baby and I made up
The houris in heaven had cup after cup

The power the rulers in order to chase
Have badly divided the human race

Carry the burden since no one can
Of love; then God has given it to man

As a symbol of love that the mystics seek
Put God the mole on her rosy cheek

On earth we surely can go astray
If Adam in Eden could lose his way

A candle may have the burning desire
But it's the moth that catches the fire

And look, how HAFIZ, with infinite pride
Adorned has he his poetry's bride

73

Dil e mun ba dour e rooyat zay chaman faraagh daarad

Whenever I see your beautiful face
The flowers all lose their beauty and grace

On me your curls, when they try to prey
The glow of your face lets them get away

Your raven locks, when my heart they steal
The light of your cheeks they use with zeal

A woman's beauty they always treasure
Though mystics forsake the worldly pleasure

O bring the wine with a marching band
The tulips are waiting with cup in hand

When a crow replaces a nightingale
With grief my heart begins to fail

Without you, darling, when I feel lovelorn
Like a candle I weep from night to morn

And in your absence when he feels morose
Your HAFIZ cares not for the tulip or rose

74

Dar azal purtoo e husnat zay tajalli dam zad

The beauty came first, and then the desire
And the love then set the whole world on fire

Abode in the angels, when love couldn't find
It made its home in the humankind

Came soon the hate to stake its claim
But a bolt from Heaven set it aflame

To capture love, then the reason tried
But Heaven its prayer promptly denied

Her chin has a dimple as deep as a well
He never got out, who into it fell

My rivals from fate got joy and bliss
Of sorrow and pain, I got the abyss

In order to see His glory and grace
God made His mirror the human face

But when HAFIZ fell in love with her
The wrath of fate he did incur

75

Doash aagahi zay yaar e safarkarda daad baad

Go find, O breeze, my departed friend
And say a message, O please do send

My heart is a captive of her curly hair
And now for its home, it does not care

When see I flowers, with beauty and grace
Remind me they do of her lovely face

When hyacinth does wave in the air
Reminded am I of her curly hair

Without her oh, how I cry and cry
I moan, and groan, and gasp, and sigh

Though the pain of parting is too much for me
The thought of her coming is a source of glee

And when I think of my friends' advice
I find it precious and above any price

And when I remember her days with me
My heart does become like a stormy sea

Though pain of parting isn't easy to bear
I lose not hope and do not despair

Because, by nature, you're noble and pure
God loves you, HAFIZ, you can be sure

76

Dar aan hawa keh juz burq andar talab nabaashad

You can't have love without the fire
And body and soul it consumes entire

When you're in love, you can't complain
And you have nothing but sorrow and pain

There is no love without rejection
And hate is also a part of affection

You need no power; you need no wealth
Love wants courage, not strength or health

Where the sun seems like a speck of dirt
You be not rude, and don't be curt

Can make you eternal no earthly wine
What you really need is the spirit divine

But you can't have, HAFIZ, a paramour
You have no money; you're too poor

77

Dilam juz mehr e mehrooyaan tareeqay bar namigeerad

Chase not the beauties, O heart of mine
Control your yen and do not pine

I have the need, and you have the pride
So by any measure, the gap is wide

With snares and traps, I like the way
Using your curls, you made me your prey

O queen of mine, do not say no
For I have no other place to go

The liquid fire that's called the wine
Hidden I carry in the gown of mine

To sell me wine anywhere in town
No barman accepts my mystic's gown

I should be burning this worthless gown
It makes me feel that I'm a clown

O fill my cup with the ruby wine
To make it tolerable, this life of mine

Rail not, O preacher, against romance
Let's all go out and sing and dance

O preacher, listen to the sound of music
It cheers the healthy and heals the sick

And like a candle, my tongue has fire
And yet no one can it ever inspire

From love, they say, I should refrain
But I simply think they're all insane

The ways of topers are not so bizarre
Them God has made the way they are

Your verses, O HAFIZ, we have been told
Are worth as much as the gems and gold

78

Damay baa gham baser burden jahaan yaksar nameearzad

Nothing can make up for a moment's pain
Let's sell my gown and buy champagne

But in the pubs, they would not touch
Alas, my gown is not worth much

Oh, full of headache is the royal crown
I'd rather wear the cap of a clown

They would not let me near her gate
I'm not worth the dirt of her estate

When an army of lovers she does regale
To keep them yearning, she wears a veil

The rewards in Heaven indeed are fine
But they cannot equal a cup of wine

In Persia, his life no one spends
If it is not for the love of friends

It looked too easy, but now I can see
Pearls don't make up for the perils of the sea

And only contentment provides relief
And nothing is worth a moment's grief

O HAFIZ, yourself do not debase
Gold cannot pay for the loss of face

79
Dostaan dukhtar e raz toba zay mastoori kard

The daughter of wine has dropped her veil
On the censor, it seems, she did prevail

Though keen and eager, I don't know why
In the company of topers, she's still very shy?

The people are tipsy, and there's full moon
And the singers are singing a beautiful tune

I should get married to the daughter of vine
It's time she leaves the vat's confine

The preacher's gown is stained with wine
So the topers now he cannot malign

The rose is flirting with the nightingale
So come, my darling, and bring some ale

Modesty, HAFIZ, is a wonderful thing
And bad is pride even for a king

80

Darakht e dosti banshaan keh kaam e dil ba baar aarad

Love and friendship are things divine
And hate is truly the devil's design

When in the tavern, be like a toper
And be not loud; it's not proper

The company of women you ought to keep
For pleasures in it there are to reap

My life is empty, and I'm glum
I pray to God to make you come

O give me a garden with eternal bloom
I'm sick and tired of the winter's gloom

My wounded heart is in your care
So tell your lips to please repair

It's also burdened by pain and sorrow
Your lips' red wine it wants to borrow

Your HAFIZ, though old, is young at heart
So stay with him and don't ever part

81

Doash az janaab e Aasif paik e bashaarat aamad

Solomon's courier has finally come
With the blessing of the premier of his kingdom

In my core of being, pour some wine
To mend the wounded heart of mine

Whatever is said in praise of my sweetie
Can't do justice to her grace and beauty

O cover my flaws with a mystic's gown
Or she will think that I am a clown

Oh, how she lowers the women's pride
When over the beauties she does preside

And admire I so much a lowly ant
When a king on throne it tries to supplant

O heart, beware; you're going to die
When hit by the dart of her saucy eye

The court of the king is like a sea
It's full of pearls wherever you see

O HAFIZ, your stains you cannot erase
Without the help of the royal grace

82

Dilay keh ghaibnumaist o jaam e Jum daarad

A heart that has the magic bowl
Like Jum, it is in full control

When giving your heart, beware, beware!
Give not to someone who does not care

The ravage of winter, she hasn't seen
Like cypress, my gal is evergreen

The night is cool, and there's full moon
Let's take our money and go to a saloon

Aware of secrets we'll never be
And life will remain a mystery

Before it saw her, my heart was aloof
But now it says it made a goof

But though she's lovely, bright, and witty
She is not very kind; she has no pity

A mystic like HAFIZ, it's hard to believe
That so many idols he keeps up his sleeve

83

Roo bar rahash nihaadam o bar mun guzar nakard

I waited and waited, but she didn't come
Of me she cared not what will become

My flood of tears was of no avail
On a heart of stone it couldn't prevail

My cries of pain no one could take
Except for her, they were all awake

When at her feet, I wanted to die
Before I could do so, she said good-bye

O please, dear God, take care of her
In safety she's just an amateur

To her, there's nothing one could deny
For her, there's no one who wouldn't die

From the eyes of hers, my wounded heart
Is always waiting for another dart

Your story of love, O HAFIZ my dear
Is so exciting; we all love to hear

84

Raseed muzhda keh ayyaam e gham na khaahad maand

Like joy, your pain will also pass
And stay you won't in this morass

By making me subject to disdain
My rival in respect will not gain

If lovers, you decide to kill them all
There'll be no one left to call you a doll

O share your wealth with the meek and poor
For one day your money will be no more

Enjoy the company of the moth, O flame
For in the morning it won't be the same

The angel of God has brought the news
Will get His mercy whoever pursues

And there is something you can't deny
That good is eternal; it will not die

Endure with patience, and do not complain
Your pain forever will not remain

In the court of Jum, they used to say
His cup will live, but the rest will decay

To the cup of wine you hold on fast
Forever, O HAFIZ, your pain won't last

85

Rooz e hijaan o shab e furqat e yaar aakhir shud

The pain of parting has come to an end
My star, it seems, has begun to ascend

In the darkness deep I see the dawn
The sun is rising, and the fog is gone

The distress of night and the trouble of heart
It seems they're all going to depart

May you, O maid, live happy and long
Bring for my headache something strong

Gone is the winter, with its baleful thorn
To allow the flowers of the spring be born

How could the fate, so mean and base
Let the mirth and joy the pain replace?

And the morn of hope, so shiny and bright
Has just come out of the veil of night

And whatever troubles I had with fate
Her coming has made them all dissipate

The bitterness soon of the winter wind
The coming of spring will all rescind

Though no one cares what happens to you
With woes, O HAFIZ, I'm glad you're through

86

Zaahid e khilwatnasheen doesh ba maikhaana shud

The preacher last night was in the bar
From mosque to tavern it isn't too far

And when he saw my infidel
To the piety the preacher said farewell

My beloved of youth when I saw in my dream
With joy this old man began to scream

When day and night, I shed my tears
Like a pearl on my lash, my tear appears

To a nightingale does his flower's desire
What does to the moth the candle's fire

Oh, intoxicated become the guys
Whenever they see the barmaid's eyes

The topers, the preacher, who used to malign
Look, how he himself now drinks the wine

And look how HAFIZ, who drinks the wine
Goes looking for God from shrine to shrine

87

Zahay khajista zamaanay keh yaar baaz aamad

One day I hope you'll come again
And you'll choose to ease my pain

I'm waiting and hoping that you'll one day
Per chance decide to come this way

Ever since my heart is trapped in your hair
It has no peace; it has no prayer

My heart is yearning to be your prey
O huntress, use your eyes to slay

Hope you'll stop this horsing around
And play with me on a level ground

Suffers the winter a nightingale
For the day, the rose when it'll hail

I also endure the sorrow and pain
Hoping one day you'll come again

But it's too much, says HAFIZ, to ask of fate
That someday you will become my mate

88

Saalha daftar e ma dar gro e sehba bood

For years, our books were pledged to the pub
Of teaching and learning, the pub was the hub

The keeper of the bar was a wise old man
Our capers and pranks he would not ban

And beautiful maids were also there
Of topers like us they took good care

So lovely were lasses who came to saloon
That they made jealous even the moon

Of preachers' faults, though we knew a lot
Allowed we were to censure them not

We used to wash our books with wine
Their contents, we thought, were all asinine

So sad sometimes was the singer's tune
That the people cried all over saloon

But came when HAFIZ, with all his money
The barman knew his money was funny

89

Saalha dil talab e jaam e Jum az ma meekard

Oh, my heart was looking for the magic bowl
When it was there, built in his soul

It was like an oyster asking for a pearl
Something it could easily unfurl

Still I went to the keeper of the bar
In solving the riddles, he is a star

Merrily holding he was the cup
Watching the whole world, down and up

When asked, he said he got his bowl
Before the Lord could heavens unroll

He said the reason had a magic show
Could fool it Moses if he didn't know

The answer you need only mystics know
The wisdom you seek only they can bestow

Or go to Gabriel; he'll do the feat
The miracles of Jesus only he can repeat

About her curls, when I asked him outright
They're HAFIZ, he said, like the long dark night

90

Sarv e chama'an e mun chira mail e chaman nameekunad

The spring has come, and the flowers are here
Oh, what a beautiful atmosphere

My heart is tangled in her curly hair
But happy it is, and has no care

A bow is her brow, and gaze an arrow
And the safety margin is very, very narrow

With hyacinths and violets everywhere
I can't help thinking of her curly hair

Go find, O breeze, my maiden fair
And bring with you the scent of her hair

Complain when I do of her cruel locks
Care she does not, and only mocks

She even says, for her beautiful ears
There won't be pearls without my tears

The breeze came back without her scent
And told me sorry, she wouldn't relent

Still my heart does long for her
It has no doubts; it doesn't demur

But HAFIZ says, since I don't take advice
He is sure one day I'll pay the price

91

Saharam doulat e baidaar ba baaleen aamad

The lady luck came in the morning and said
   "Your love is here; so get out of bed

"Look jolly and fit, and drink some wine
   Before you welcome this darling divine

"And thank your star; to make you her beau
   From Khutan has comes a musky doe

"Your tears have reddened your pallid cheek
   Your moan has helped a lover so meek

"But watch you out, and restrain your love
   For she is an eagle, and you're a dove"

O barmaid dear, let's all celebrate
   My rivals are gone with all their hate

This wine, O maid, give me some more
   And heal with it my bleeding sore

In order to mourn the malice of fate
Even clouds are shedding the tears of late

My wounded heart one has to praise
It yearns for the arrows of a charming gaze

Singing your ode is the nightingale
   Let's drink, O HAFIZ, go get some ale

92

Sitaaraay badarakhsheed o maah e majlis bood

A star from Heaven came down to earth
In the Arabian Desert, he took his birth

He couldn't read, and couldn't write
But teach he could the brightest of bright

An edifice great he built with skill
And a mission Divine he did fulfill

My love has made me so dignified
That over the topers I now preside

Oh, wipe not wine from your juicy lip
And give my lips a chance to sip

O please, my darling, do not flirt
Lest creed and logic your lovers desert

They'll eat, and drink, and dance, and sing
And become they'll the envy of the king

Their lovesick hearts will be ever more sick
They'll yell, and scream, and howl, and kick

They'll lose their faith, and belief, and creed
And advice and counsel they'll not heed

And the troubles you have, O HAFIZ, I think
Are because you chase the girls and drink

93
Saaqi ar baada az ein dast ba jaam andaazad

Oh, the way she pours and serves the wine
In it a mystics can see the Divine

Her mole is a bait and the curl a snare
O wise old man, beware, beware!

When the day does wear the veil of night
For drinking and dancing the time is right

In the day you toil, and work, and think
When the night falls, you drink and drink

So that you know not, when you go to bed
Where is your turban and where is your head

And when your head is on her feet
You become a part of a great elite

If once the preacher drinks the wine
The topers he will never, never malign

But with censor, O HAFIZ, don't ever drink
For after he drinks, he raises a stink

94

Sahar bulbul hikaayat baa saba kard

Said the singing bird to the morning breeze
That the love of a flower is a terrible disease

I deeply love and admire a beauty
Who does some good as a matter of duty

May God you bless, O morning breeze
You soothe my pain and bring me ease

Complain I do not against my foes
It's the friends who give me all my woes

And it is the rose that causes the pain
Against the thorn, one cannot complain

So cries and cries the nightingale
And everyone else is hearty and hale

From a beautiful girl expect no favor
Whatever you get you learn to savor

With all her beauty, and charm, and grace
She uses her hair to hide her face

But Kamaal, my patron, is always so kind
A nicer person is difficult to find

So I care not, HAFIZ, what people think
I'll defy them all, and openly drink

95

Saaqi andar qadeham baaz mai e gulgoon kard

Tonight she gave me a wonderful wine
And something with it she did combine

Though wine she gave to everyone
With me she tried to have some fun

Nothing it was but a total rout
It took a sip to knock me out

The wine she gave was crimson red
It seems it was from a heart that bled

A wounded heart I haven't got
It's all in pieces, and it's all shot

It isn't my heart that I cannot find
My love has made me even lose my mind

And in fact, O HAFIZ, you aren't so wise
You too are a captive of her charming eyes

96
Sapeedadam kah saba boo e dostaan geerad

In the morning breeze, the scent of your hair
It makes the garden with Eden compare

The sound of music when the preachers hear
Of drinking and dancing they lose their fear

From the veil of night, in the heavenly spheres
The sun comes out, and the morning appears

The shining eagle, with its golden rays
On the crow of the night it comes and preys

Let's go to the park with the wine straight
Where, cups in hand, the tulips wait

Let's go and see the flowers of spring
And hear the birds as they wing and sing

The sun will set in the garden soon
Let's sit and drink under the golden moon

And let's ask HAFIZ his verses to sing
For among the poets, he is the king

97

Shaahidaan ger dilbari zeensaan kunand

The beauties, whenever with preachers flirt
Them faith and creed instantly desert

And when they ever hear them sing
The houris in Heaven swing and swing

Their radiant face, when the lovers see
Contain they cannot their ecstasy

But when they become cruel and severe
The lovers shed blood with every tear

And since they love with heart and soul
On lovers the beauties have full control

And those who shed in tears the blood
They aren't impressed by the biblical flood

The lovers on their death, when they come to see
Easy they make their mortality

And when they see on the cheek a mole
Gladly the lovers sacrifice the soul

So cheer up, O heart; your pain will pass
You will get out of this morass

A lover, O HAFIZ, shouldn't complain
For there is no gain without the pain

98

Soofi ar baada ba andaaza khurad nooshash baad

Drink, O mystics, only so much wine
Anything more you must decline

To the mystics wine those who give
May they forever with lovers live

And to her lovers, a girl who's kind
An eternal bliss may the darling find

The eyes, which lovers with arrows slay
May they forever be happy and gay

My lips, the victims of her prejudice
May her juicy lips some day they kiss

Her lovers, a girl who does disdain
O may she never feel the pain

My faults, the preacher who does so hate
May never he be a victim of fate

Since love, O HAFIZ, has made you renowned
The girl you love deserves to be crowned

99

Saba waqt e sahar booay zay zulf e yaar meeaawurd

When brought the breeze the scent of her hair
My wounded heart it helped repair

In her golden tresses, when the air got caught
It gave up the musk of Tartar it brought

And in the terrace, when it saw her moon
The sun hid behind the clouds at noon

Though she is cruel, heartless, and callous
She can also be kind, sweet, and zealous

For this or that, I do not fret
I take from her whatever I get

Her if I could tear from my heart away
I would be happy, and jolly, and gay

With her charming eyes, needless to say
She's the huntress, and I'm the prey

With her long and curly braided hair
In chains she drags me everywhere

But when she sings, and gives me a drink
I lose my head and the power to think

When HAFIZ I saw, with a bottle of wine
Since he is a mystic, I thought it was fine

100

Saba ba tehniat e peer e maifaroosh aamad

The morning breeze has brought the news
It's time to sing, and dance, and booze

Blooming are flowers with fragrance in air
And flying and singing are birds everywhere

The trees are wearing their green attire
And flowers have set the garden on fire

An angel came and said it to me
That jolly and happy it's time to be

It's time to love and not to fight
For the devil in us has taken the flight

Look, iris, the talker, who's such a riot
God only knows why is it so quiet?

And in this lovely atmosphere
I don't know why is the preacher here?

With us I hope he is in sync
He might have come to have a drink

And HAFIZ has also left the shrine
I bet he's coming to have some wine

101

Aks e roo e to keh dar aaiena jaam uftaad

Her beauty's image when the mystic saw
Dazzled he was; he was in awe

Having seen her beauty, he became devout
In the glory of God it left no doubt

When from her face, she lifted the veil
The faith was happy, and the reason hale

The visage the mystic saw in the wine
It was the barmaid's image divine

Meaning of love only mystics know
It's a mystery for the ordinary Joe

A captive of love is truly free
How very blessed is a tramp like me

Only pure of heart can see the light
An evil eye is devoid of sight

He stands alone, and he stands above
Blessed is the one who dies for love

And from her dimple into her hair
Went my heart from a well to a snare

O preacher, I am leaving your shrine
From now on, it'll be women and wine

From mosque to the bar, if I go straight
It is my destiny; it is my fate

To and fro, I go with the flow
Round and round in the world I go

Though as a mystic I'm not alone
Among the topers I'm well known

All mystics, HAFIZ, like the wine
But I'm the one who people malign

102
Ishqat na sarsariest keh az sar badar shawad

My love of her is a serious thing
Although for her it's just a fling

With mother's milk it went into me
Out of my heart it will never be

The pangs of love you must endure
They get much worse if you try to cure

All night I cry and cry with pain
My moans and groans I can't contain

With the flood of tears that I can't abate
The country of Iraq I can irrigate

Covers her face with hair when she
Behind the clouds, the moon I see

And whenever I ask her for a kiss
She tells me no, with an emphasis

Thinking of her, when I take a drink
About my rival, I don't ever think

And her on my grave, O HAFIZ, I'll greet
By getting right up, and kissing her feet

103

Ghalaam e nargis e mast e to taajdaaraanand

A slave of your eyes is truly a king
The wine of your lips is the real thing

Your shyness, my crying did secrets reveal
Though lovers tell never however they feel

In your locks the captives, O you should see
They are as wretched as they can be

When I see the violets, I feel so bad
Being jealous of your curls, they look very sad

O tell my rival not to be so proud
And not to be lusty, and boisterous, and loud

I'm not the only one who lauds your cheek
There're millions and millions your rose who seek

My rivals laugh; with blisters I cry
I go on foot while they all ride by

O Come to the pub, you'll be close to God
In the shrine the sheik is a total fraud

After his death, in Heaven he lives
For God a sinner, he always forgives

And a captive of your locks though HAFIZ may be
As a prisoner there he is truly free

104

Qatl e ein khasta ba shamsheer e to taqdeer nabood

My dying by your sword was not to be
Though you were in favor of killing me

Pity from your beauty I don't expect
On it my sighs have little effect

I left the mosque and went to the bar
The views of the preacher were so very bizarre

A captive of curls who wants to be free
He is as crazy as crazy can be

No cypress in the park is at all like you
Even beauties like you, in pictures, are few

Remembering your tresses, I don't know why
All night long I cry and cry?

I moan and groan; I gasp and sigh
Without you, darling, I'll surely die

Oh, in your absence, my life is hell
And HAFIZ knows it all too well

105

Like pearls my tears drop from my eyes
Like stars they twinkle until sunrise

The pain of parting has made me frail
My bones are bent; my face is pale

And a yearning lover to mortify
The crescent, like a dagger, holds the sky

Oh, when she holds the cup to her lip
The wine looks red when she takes a sip

Her teeth, O HAFIZ, just look at them
Each one is like a pearl or a gem

106

Kalk e mushkeen e to roozay keh zay ma yaad kunad

If one day she would write to me
God will give her the Heaven's key

Greeting from Selma, O breeze, if you bring
For it I will give you just about anything

May God guide and show her the way
So that she comes, and comes to stay

Her love has given me nothing but strife
No doctor now can save my life

She is above and beyond my praise
Her beauty needs no make-up, no glaze

But if someday she is nice to me
God will give her bliss and glee

Yes, piety is good for a noble king
But justice from him is everything

Living in Persia does not pay
In Iraq, O HAFIZ, I'll make my way

107

Kasay keh husn e rukh e dost dar nazar daarad

Whoever sees your beautiful face
Your image from his eye he can't erase

Only he can win you, and he can woo
The one who's willing to die for you

And only he can kiss your feet
The one who resigns in total defeat

Your gaze's arrows nurture my heart
But I cannot take my rival's dart

I'm sick of piety; give me some wine
In order to nourish this soul of mine

Look, how the preacher has changed his tune
Now every night he's in the saloon

The wine, he says, helps him unwind
And gives him the needed peace of mind

But this HAFIZ of ours you cannot save
His broken heart he'll take to his grave

108

Ger maifaroash hajit e rindaan rawa kunad

If the barman gives me a little bit of wine
He'll get in Heaven the spirit divine

Pray not induce, and do not deduce
Wisdom in the bar is of no use

Here, there isn't any reason or rhyme
And no one dies before his time

And if you're sad, or if you have pain
It's from God; do not complain

For the pang of love you need a stein
And with hangover drink some wine

In the glow of glory you'll shine and shine
Fidelity and faith are simply divine

When a mystic asks, do not decline
You ought to give him his share of the wine

Look, HAFIZ has died of pain and strife
Only she, who killed him, can give him the life

109
Guftam kayam dahaan o labat kaamraan kunand

When your lips – I asked – will favor me?
Whatever you say – she said – will be

I said that Egypt they ask as a price
For now – she said – that would suffice

I said – your mouth no one can kiss
She said – it's something I do not miss

I said that the idols I worship not
She smiled and said – Oh, I forgot

I said – I drown my sorrow in the wine
With a nod she said – it's just fine

I said that mystics should not drink
She said – it's not what here we think

I asked – what the old men get from a kiss
She said – it's something they really miss

I asked – my beloved when will I win?
She said - in place when your star is in

I said that HAFIZ prays for you
She said - the same the angels do

110
Gul bai rukh e yaar khush nabaashad

Without her face the flowers are nothing
And without the wine there is no spring

The lovely garden and the morning breeze
Without my darling they do not please

The lovely cypress and the charming rose
Without the birds they have the woes

The garden, the flowers, and the vintage wine
Without my baby I always decline

With all my prudence, wisdom, and reason
Without my love I am simply no one

Her sugary mouth if I cannot kiss
No lips I fancy; no mouth I miss

Your offer of life she will not touch
For her, O HAFIZ, it isn't worth much

111

Gercheh bar waaiz e shehr ein sukhan aasaan nashawad

Knows not the preacher that if you're a fraud
Become you cannot a man of God

Become a toper, if you possibly can
For if you don't drink, you aren't a man

If they are no good, you can't help them
Not every stone can become a gem

O pray to God; He'll show you the way
With help from Him you can't go astray

Sorrow and grief if you want to avert
First tell your doctor where you hurt

Don't be afraid; you will be fine
Do fall in love, for it is divine

Tomorrow – she said – I'll do your bidding
I hope to God that she wasn't kidding

May God teach her how to be good
So that she treats me as she should

Don't be afraid of giving your life
For love is full of pain and strife

With courage, O HAFIZ, it can be done
A speck of dirt can become the sun

112

Gercheh az ghamza butam zakhmay ba dil kaari kunad

With her magical eyes she wounds my heart
But practice she can also the healing art

Her lips are filled with the ruby wine
Her charming eyes are simply divine

If ever the preacher becomes like me
From taboos all he will be free

And if the singer sings my song
I'll be dancing all night long

All night I'll drink, and drown my sorrow
And for the morning, some wine I'll borrow

For my girl, O HAFIZ, I crave and pine
I wish she'd come and bring some wine

113
Ger zulf e pareeshaanat dar dast e saba uftad

Whenever her curls fly in the air
People so love them everywhere

The pangs of love I can't endure
Do I've patience; I can't be sure?

Escape I can't from the pain of mine
When blood I see in my cup of wine

With musk her hair when I try to compare
She tells fiercely – don't you dare!

I cry, and cry, and cry again
Without her, HAFIZ, I've so much pain

114
Mara ba rindi o ishq aan fuzool aeb kunad

The sheik who scorns my love of wine
Knows he not it's the fate of mine

The love and truth no preacher exalts
Instead, he's always finding faults

The barmaid lures us without restraint
Resist her cannot even a saint

The charm of the barmaid, if you do not know
In Heaven, no houri for you will go

And truly happy the topers are
If you're in doubt, just look in the bar

Like Moses to God if you want to talk
For years you shepherd Jethro's flock

The story of HAFIZ whoever hears
He can't help shedding his blood in tears

115
Mun o inkaar e sharaab ein cheh hikaayat baashad

Me not drinking, O what a lie
On such a rumor don't you rely

Me and piety, O not a chance
It's not a likely circumstance

Liquor and piety do not mix
Love and preacher – fiddlesticks!

The tavern keeper is a wise man
I take his advice whenever I can

The sheik is proud, and the toper meek
Try to guess, whom God will seek?

And HAFIZ knows not what to think
Of the man who tells him not to drink

116

Maashiraan zay hareef e shabaana yaad aareed

O forget you not your drinking friend
And how on him you could depend

Of hopes and wishes if you happen to think
Think how we used to sit and drink

The image of barmaid if you see in the drink
Remember, at us how she used to wink

And when you hear the singers sing
Think how together we used to swing

For fidelity people care not a bit
You know our world, how fickle is it

So when you go riding, don't be unkind
And think of the people you leave behind

And if you want some good to do
Think of your HAFIZ and his love for you

117
Mun o salaah o salaamat kas ein gumaan naburad

Me being pious, no, it can't be true
A thing like this a toper can't do

Don't be fooled by the gown of mine
I use it to hide my bottle of wine

O preacher, please be not so proud
Defying the fate is never allowed

Don't be deceived by the worldly shine
The peace and bliss are all in the wine

Your eyes are there to keep the watch
But they are the ones who often botch

From loving the girls if you can't abstain
You should have strength to bear the pain

And with wise men, HAFIZ, use some art
And don't you try to be so smart

118
Mara mehr e siyehchashmaan zay dil bairoon nakhahad shud

Love I'll always those eyes black
Passion for them I'll never lack

God has given me the love of wine
It's His will, and the fate of mine

My love for her is without strings
No hugs, no kisses, no sways, no swings

With a friendly barmaid and the vintage wine
Life is happy and everything is fine

So go to the bar, and become a toper
For drinking again is legal and proper

Though lovers she has quite a few
No one can love her like I do

And though my rivals are cruel and mean
I stay unruffled, and calm, and serene

I see in my wine the secret of being
Come, look in my cup; it's worth seeing

And, HAFIZ, I have no hopes, no fears
To wash my wounds I use my tears

119
Maashiraan gireh az zulf e yaar baaz kuneed

Let's untie her knotted hair
And spread its fragrance everywhere

The evil eye we cannot ignore
So let's get together, and shut the door

Let's examine, and let's explore
And listen to those who know the score

Love and friendship if one knows not
A soul in his body, he hasn't got

A lover and his love are poles apart
He's all affection; she has no heart

He may be faulty, flawed, and odd
But a man, who loves, is loved by God

The tavern keeper is a wise teacher
He always says – beware of the preacher!

From her, O HAFIZ, if I wants a reward
To me a kiss she should promptly award

120

Mara ba wasl e to ger zaan keh dastras baashad

If ever she came to live with me
I'll be as happy as I can be

If only for a moment I am with her
Over everything else, it I'll prefer

Whenever you go, you find her door
Always surrounded by lovers galore

Wherever you look, you see a flood
And lovers drowning in tears of blood

She'll wink at you and take your life
She needs no saber, no sword, no knife

One time she will be very nice to you
Next day she'll see you and won't say boo

To touch her even, you aren't allowed
She's so splendid, so lofty, so proud

Despite it all, I want her still
O HAFIZ, I love her and always will

121

Muzhda aey dil keh digar baad e saba baaz aamad

Rejoice, O heart, the news is here
The queen of Sheba is about to appear

The birds have taken up David's tone
And the flowers are sitting on Solomon's throne

Waiting in line, the tulips stand
Asking for wine, with cup in hand

Is there a mystic who can tell us why
Comes iris only to say good-bye?

For a change, the fate is kind to me
My gal's as sweet as sweet can be

And finally, after a long delay
The caravan of flowers is coming our way

And although, HAFIZ, I deserve it not
My gal for me does care a lot

122
Na her keh chehra barafroekht dilbari daanad

Not all, who are pretty, possess the splendor
Not everyone who conquers is an Alexander

Not everyone who does scowl and frown
Is fit to wear the royal crown

And a man who wears the mystic's gown
May turn out to be a dreadful clown

A lover's prospects are quite dim
In the flood of tears, if he cannot swim

I am the slave of the noble toper
With the heart of gold, who looks like a pauper

Only jewelers know the price of her mole
For it's a gem though black as coal

I love a gal who is pure like Mary
Lovely like a houri, and fairer than a fairy

A beautiful woman, though it's rare
Conquers the world, if just and fair

And a lovely girl who is not so callous
Does make the beauties angry and jealous

Perform the service without the wage
Because your master is a noble sage

The verses of HAFIZ only they appreciate
The ones who are cultured, skilled, and sedate

123

Nafas e baad e saba mushkfishaan khahad shud

The world will soon be fresh and fair
And the scent of flowers will be everywhere

The tulip will share its wine with lily
And the iris will talk but won't be silly

So with a dainty girl you lie on the lawn
And enjoy the flowers before they are gone

Sit by the water and drink some ale
And listen to the song of a nightingale

Live for today and don't be dumb
Say not tomorrow, for it may not come

Drink all you can this time of the year
For the month of fasting will soon be here

If drinking alone you feel love-sick
Console yourself with the sound of music

The preacher's advice is not worth a dime
Listen not to him; don't waste your time

Oh, how I wish she would come to her guy
O HAFIZ, if only to say good-bye

124

Her keh shud mehram e dil dar haram e yaar bamaand

If you know yourself, and know your heart
From everyone else you'll stand apart

How lucky of me that I am a toper
For arrogance and pride are so improper

The lovers come and the lovers go
But the story of mine everyone will know

To hide my faults, I use my gown
Without it surely I'll look like a clown

O love is supreme; it is so divine
In heaven and earth there's nothing so fine

In the cup what looks like the ruby wine
It's actually blood in the tears of mine

My heart will be hers, forever and ever
And change it won't, never, never, never

Though narcissus looks like a beautiful eye
When it sees her eye, it feels very shy

And like me, though mystics do love the wine
Their robes aren't pawned like the gown of mine

Her grace and elegance no picture can catch
Her charm and beauty no painting can match

And the day when, HAFIZ, I saw her hair
My heart got caught in its lovely snare

125

Her aan koo khaatir e mujmu o yaar e naazneen daarad

Anyone who conquers a dainty gal
His friend is fortune and luck his pal

Love is beyond and above our reason
And the one, who loves, does fear no one

The poor and the meek you don't disdain
For they'll inherit the Godly domain

So don't you despise the poor and the needy
Share your blessings, and don't be so greedy

Savor your strength while still you're young
For soon unto dust you'll be flung

In front of my queen when you go, O breeze
Like everyone else you fall on your knees

For curly tresses and locks has she
Her lips are as sweet as sweet can be

Her mouth is like the Solomon's seal
It has the authority and wide appeal

But if she says that HAFIZ is nothing
Tell her that he has the heart of a king

126

Her kera baa khat e sabzat sar e soda baashad

Anyone who loves your curly hair
He has no chance, he has no prayer

On Judgment Day, when he'll rise from grave
For its delicate fragrance he'll still crave

His heart will seek the shade of your hair
In order to find refuge in there

How long, how long, O precious one
This lover of yours you're going to shun

All night long, he cries and cries
With rivers flowing from his tearful eyes

So come to your HAFIZ before he dies
He's dying to see your brown eyes

127

Hergizam mehr e to az loh e dil o jaan narawad

Her love will never leave my heart
Her thought from me will never depart

Her love is rooted so deep in me
That a part of me it'll always be

Unique is she; she's one of a kind
Her picture is always in my mind

The pang of love that's in my heart
From the soul of mine it'll never part

So tangled am I in her curly hair
I have no hope; I haven't a prayer

The pain of love I can't endure
I chase the gals to find a cure

And if like HAFIZ you don't want to be
Don't fall in love, and that's the key

128

Her keh o yak sar e moo pand e mara goash kunad

If you are going to follow me
A slave of a gal you'll surely be

And if you ever kissed her lip
Only ruby wine you'll ever sip

In the park whenever she takes a walk
So awed is iris, it cannot talk

Her curly hair, when it flies in the air
The lovers get trapped in its lovely snare

Though pain of parting I cannot bear
I forget it, HAFIZ, when she is there

129
Yaad baad aan keh nihaanat nazaray baa ma bood

There was a time when you were kind
The pact we had was sealed and signed

And even when you were cross with me
You were always as sweet as sweet can be

And when you wore your stylish hat
Oh, how on its face did moon fall flat

Your shining face, it was so bright
That lovers, like moths, were there all night

Your lips, when covered they were with wine
Oh, how I used to wipe them with mine

And in your salon when we used to dine
The sauciest thing there was the wine

And in your chamber when we drank alone
God was there as your chaperone

And when we sat and drank at the bar
Everything we wanted wasn't very far

And your HAFIZ from you took his cue
His verses all were inspired by you

130
Yaari andar kas nameebeenaem yaaraan ra cheh shud

Gone is camaraderie; there is no friend
On no one now can you ever depend

The flowers are withering, and the spring is gone
The leaves are falling, and the freeze is on

The birds in the garden do not sing
There is no scent for the breeze to bring

There's no kindness, no help, no pity
The picture you see is not very pretty

In the bar the topers are full of gloom
The ladies of the night are losing their bloom

Indifference in faces you see everywhere
What happens to you, people don't care

Apathy and scorn are commonplace
Whatever happened to mercy and grace?

We know, O HAFIZ, you have the woes
But the answers you seek, nobody knows

131

Yaad baad aan keh sar e koo e to am manzil bood

There was a time, I lived in her street
And used to kiss the dirt of her feet

My way to her heart I could easily find
I had on my tongue what was in her mind

And what was above and beyond my brain
My feelings of love could always explain

And what, in her absence, was hard to bear
Became very pleasant when she was there

And I used to think that she was all mine
But alas, she had another design

For old time's sake, I went to the bar
Instead of wine, there was blood in the jar

About pangs of love when I asked my doc
What he said to me was all poppycock

Oh, when I think of Ishaq, the king
I feel he was like the breeze of spring

Yes, HAFIZ, he was like a happy bird
Of the mighty hawk who had never heard

132
Yaad baad aan keh zay ma waqt e safar yaad nakard

She left and didn't even say good-bye
On whom, dear God, can I ever rely?

And she, who is kind as kind can be
This old, old slave she wouldn't free

Hoping that someday she'll hear my cry
I moan, and groan, and sob, and sigh

And tears of blood I shed and shed
Until my clothes are stained all red

In the garden I sit, and wait, and wail
Like, in the autumn, a nightingale

But when I see her radiant face
I cannot resist its beauty and grace

And though of my love she's quite aware
What happens to me, she doesn't really care

But the verses of HAFIZ whoever hears
He can't help crying and shedding tears

133

Aey zoaq e shehd e laal e to dar kaam e mun lazeez

O yummy is the taste of your luscious lips
From them, when you talk, the honey drips

Around the pearls of your precious teeth
Your lips with rubies do form a wreath

Whenever I talk of your sugary lips
My words taste like the chocolate chips

And the scent of your curly fragrant hair
To the musk of Khutan I can easily compare

But in your absence when I cry and cry
Like stars my tears do fall from my eye

O let me nibble on your dimpled chin
My heartache needs no aspirin

And for a lovesick HAFIZ nothing can replace
The glowing radiance of your beautiful face

134
Aey guftogoo e laal e to dar kaam e jaan lazeez

Tasty is the talk of her juicy lip
Mention her mouth and my heart does flip

Like drops of milk are her lovely teeth
Over which her lips form a sugary sheath

My roasted heart she comes to rob
For wine goes better with shish kabob

But whenever she's nice, the world looks kind
And anything nicer would be hard to find

And when with a glance she wounds my heart
My heart rejoices and savors her dart

And it tastes so sweet that I repeat and repeat
Her name forever like a parakeet

And, HAFIZ, you'll also find it sweet
When you go and kiss the dirt of her feet

135
Ila aey tooti e gooya e israar

O you, all-knowing parakeet
May you always have your sweetmeat

With a heart so happy, and a head so smart
You're so much like my sweetheart

No problem there's that you can't resolve
There is no puzzle that you cannot solve

O let's go down and drink at the bar
And count our blessings, and thank our star

Enjoy the music and all the romance
Drunk or sober, let's get up and dance

Oh, whatever the barmaid does put in the cup
It turns our minds all downside up

Though reason and wisdom do make us shine
The love is eternal; it's so very divine

In wealth and power put not our trust
For the mighty kings end up all in the dust

The feet of mystics we should go and touch
They mean a lot but say not much

Go not to the preacher, for knows he not
He means very little but says a lot

And chase not the girls, it's not so funny
For all these beauties are after our money

But the master of ours is so very kind
A man like him is difficult to find

Indebted I am to Mansur, the king
For me, O HAFIZ, he's everything

136
Aey khurram az faroagh e rukhat laalazaar e umr

Your radiant face makes my life bright
Come back, for the spring is taking the flight

My tears are falling like torrential rain
Like thunder and lightning is my dreadful pain

When life to a lover only you can give
Without you, darling, how can I live?

With lips so red, and mouth so small
Your mouth a rosebud I'll have to call

When peril and danger I see everywhere
No wonder I have such terrible despair

You if I could only for a moment see
So dark and empty my life wouldn't be

And if some night I do fall asleep
Wake up when I, I weep and weep

And when you wouldn't even look at me
You leave me in torment and in agony

But I, your HAFIZ, when I write the verse
I make you the queen of the universe

137

Aey saba nik'hatay az khaak e dar e yaar biyaar

Go, bring good news from her, O breeze
Some scent of her body bring also please

Some happy tidings do bring from her
And the mystical secrets on me confer

Bring also the scent of her breath for me
For there's nothing that it can't remedy

Her, in the street, if you happen to meet
Bring also with you the dirt of her feet

Of being without her I am so fed up
Do bring her image in the magic cup

And on your way if you find some dust
In her passageway, bring it you must

About the spring I haven't yet heard
So bring good news to this captive bird

Her absence has made my life so bitter
So bring a sweet word or two from her

This heart of mine is totally insane
Go, get her curls and make me a chain

For the foolish ones I do not fall
I love so much my crafty doll

And though being a HAFIZ I live in a shrine
My gown is full of the stains of wine

138

Aey bar umeed e wasl e to mouqoof kaar e umr

O come for a while and be with me
May God you live for a century

Even for a moment when you're with me
I'm as happy as I possibly can be

Without you living is not worthwhile
And being this lonely is not my style

You are my life; I love you no end
Although on life one cannot depend

But since I've been living without you
I have been doing nothing but boohoo

And I have nothing but pain and strife
But as HAFIZ says, "But then this is life"

139

Baad az ein hargiz nabeenad heetch maikhaaray digar

No one in the pub will ever see
A barmaid like ours and a toper like me

Oh, this maid of ours we all so adore
And never stop saying - some more, some more

I sell my gown, not piety
So don't be so critical, O preacher, of me

A lover forever sheds blood in tears
And bleeding to death he never fears

This turban of HAFIZ O don't you scorn
It's something to treasure, even though it's worn

140

Deegar zay shaakh e sarv e sahi bulbul e saboor

Said the bird to flower, "My sweetie pie
May God protect you from the evil eye

"Be not so proud; just savor your bloom
And try to dispel your lover's gloom"

The preacher is drooling over a houri in Heaven
But in the pub we have, not one, but seven

About her absence I can't complain
There can be no joy without the pain

Others are merry, joyous, and happy
But I feel sad, and crummy, and crappy

Let's go to the bar and dance and drink
Of sin and virtue let us not think

And, HAFIZ my boy, don't you complain
Without the loss you can't have gain

141

Rooay banma o wujood e khudam az yaad babar

Oh, how her eyes do mesmerize
And how they soothe and hypnotize

My passion for her is like a storm
Of troubles and woes it has a swarm

Burning in my heart is a terrible fire
My tears are flowing; my plight is dire

To win in love, one needs a teacher
But please don't ever consult the preacher

Oh, like daggers are her long eyelashes
With them my heart she stabs and slashes

She does not like to see me crying
But I hope she comes when I'm dying

Our tavern keeper is a wonderful guy
On his advice one can always rely

I would like to go and live in her street
So whenever she passes, I would kiss her feet

And I would smell the scent of her hair
When in and out I breathe the air

And, HAFIZ, I'll keep my eyes dry
For she gets upset whenever I cry

142
Saaqia maaya e sharaab biyaar

Bring back my youth, my vigor, my shine
And do not forget the ruby wine

The pangs of love it helps us endure
Whether young or old, it has our cure

The wine is the sun and the cup is moon
And a cup with wine is like moon at noon

Drink and dance and let's not worry
Call in the singers, and we must hurry

Listen to the heart and not to reason
For drinking and dancing are now in season

My heart is aflame with a burning desire
Go, get some wine and put out the fire

Without the roses I can always do
But wine I need when I'm feeling blue

The sound of birds I can do without
But without the wine I'm all washed out

Of sin and virtue I do not think
Right or wrong, I must've a drink

And while awake I scheme and scheme
But have her I can't, except in my dream

But when I am sober, I am in a funk
So I drink and drink until I'm drunk

Oh, give your HAFIZ a drink or two
And don't you preach, whatever you do

143
Sarv e baalabuland e khush raftaar

She's tall, and slim, and slender, and neat
To watch her strolling is a real treat

She neatly stole the heart of mine
Whatever she does, she does by design

Her golden curls when they fly in the air
Smell their fragrance you can everywhere

So lovely, so sweet, so comely is she
If only she had some fidelity

I'll never complain of that or this
If she would only give me a kiss

Oh, how I love her beautiful eyes
They charm, they soothe, the mesmerize

And for her affection, Oh, how I crave
Though, HAFIZ, I am just a poor slave

144
Saba zay manzil e jaanaan guzar dareegh madaar

Do go to her place, O breeze of spring
And happy news for her lover bring

Tell her that she is a beautiful rose
And I, her nightingale, have a lot of woes

With you a message she ought to send
For after all I am a very old friend

A friend, a lover, a mystic am I
To me a favor she shouldn't deny

Singing her praise I go everywhere
So she should be nice: it's only fair

I do not ask for gold or money
I only want her to be my honey

With her so sugary, so luscious, so sweet
Why not some sugar for her parakeet?

As a mystic who sees so much in trance
Why doesn't she also give me a chance?

When she was budding, she was my rose
Now blooming, she wouldn't let me be close

So ever since, HAFIZ, she said good-bye
I can do nothing but sit and cry

145

Eid ast o moesam e gul o yaaraan dar intazaar

The fasting is over; it's time to dine
And toast our king with the vintage wine

I gave up drinking but not for long
For not to drink in the spring is wrong

My life is all that for him I can give
And it'll be his as long as I live

May you, O king, rule the earth and sky
May God protect you from the evil eye

And when you drink your ruby wine
I hope you'll hear some verses of mine

To the worldly pleasures do not succumb
And follow the lead of the noble Jum

And don't you forget, O king of mine
That love is noble, high, and divine

So with HAFIZ drink and have no fear
For the fasting is over, and the spring is here

146

Ger bawad umr ba maikhaana rawam baar e digar

I'll go, if lucky, to the bar again
In the service of topers I'll there remain

And there I'll go with flowing tears
To wash and clean its door and stairs

But if people there for me didn't care
I'll pack my bag and go elsewhere

My love of beauties is full of strife
For a change I want a peaceful life

If only I could with fate conspire
I'd find an angel that I so desire

Secret I'll keep my love affair
Though keeping it hidden is very, very rare

And if she left me for any reason
Love and romance, I'll forever shun

I know that the fate is not very kind
A way to hurt me it will always find

But in this, HAFIZ, I'm not alone
There're millions like me who moan and groan

147
Naseehatay kunamat bashnoo o bahaana mageer

Listen to me and take my advice
For it will be useful, and very, very nice

Do fall in love with beautiful girls
Look in their eyes, and play with their curls

Nothing in life has a greater worth
Love is supreme in heaven and earth

Sit with your gal and sing a song
And if you've a flute, bring it along

There is nothing wrong in having a drink
About sin and virtue don't ever think

Your loving heart, restrain you not
And give love all whatever you've got

The rights and wrongs you do not debate
And do not worry about luck or fate

My drinking so often I've tried to forgo
But to the maid of the bar I can't say no

O barman, please pour me some wine
For I cannot forget this girl of mine

I'm so dried up, and she is so green
I'm so old; she's only fourteen

I could not resist her golden hair
And now I'm caught in its deadly snare

Millions of rivals have I everywhere
But I have the help of Asif, the fair

So fall in love, and don't be awed
For this I've heard from an angel of God

And go to the bar and take my advice
For the barmaids there are lovely and nice

And verses of HAFIZ there you sing
For among the poets he is the king

148

Yusuf e gumgashta baaz aayad ba kinaan gham makhur

One day your Joseph will surely be back
Always, O Jacob, it won't look so black

Your gloomy heart will feel much better
Forever the pain and sorrow won't occur

One day for sure the flowers will come
And the birds and the bees won't be so glum

You will not be always in such a bind
Forever your fate won't be unkind

Nobody knows what the future holds
You'll be surprised when it unfolds

Don't be so hopeless, and do not despair
You are bound to find some friends who care

A bird who loves to kiss a rose
The prick of the thorn it also knows

The pain of her parting and your rival's dart
Won't be forever; don't take it to heart

The boat may be shaky; there may be a storm
If your guide is Noah, it's going to perform

Your road may be risky; it may be long
Have faith in God; you won't go wrong

So worry not, HAFIZ, you silly clod
Just read your Quran, and pray to God

149

Aey sarv e naaz e husn keh khush meerawi ba naaz

O gorgeous one, when you proudly walk
To see your splendor your lovers flock

Since God has made you splendid and proud
To scorn your lovers you're justly allowed

And if I want to play with your hair
Of its deadly snare I'm fully aware

And if I want to kiss your cheek
I am a moth and a flame I seek

And ever since I've been in your street
In there I've found my peaceful retreat

The arch of your brow ever since I've seen
To pray in the mosque, I'm not very keen

And ever since the preacher has seen the pub
It has come to be his favorite hub

And HAFIZ loves wine with his heart and soul
Ever since he has drunk from the magic bowl

150

Ba raah e maikada ushshaaq raast dar tag o taaz

On the way to the bar the topers feel
Like all those pilgrims, a furious zeal

I like to hide my pains, my fears
But what do I do with my telltale tears

Oh, love wants beauty and beauty love
They're meant for each other like hand and glove

Day and night I live in her street
For there I find a peaceful retreat

She is my goddess, my love, my friend
She is my beginning and she is the end

For me, of life she is the fountainhead
For in her absence I'm worse than dead

And though I see no hope, no sign
I feel someday she's going be mine

I try to hide the way I feel
But my love for her I cannot conceal

O HAFIZ, this love is a deadly game
For I'm the moth, and she is the flame

151
Bia o kashti e ma dar shat e sharaab andaaz

Come, bring some wine and then behold
How it revives the young and the old

A cup won't do for the sorrow of mine
Drown it instead in a vat of wine

In the rosy wine when I drown my woes
I put much envy in the heart of rose

Do bring some wine in the medicine cart
To soothe, O nurse, my woeful heart

And if at night you would like sunshine
Just lift the veil from the face of the wine

Oh, bury my body not in the ground
In a barrel of wine I want to be drowned

To escape from prison your HAFIZ won't dare
If you bind him tight with your braided hair

152
Rooz o aish o tarab o eid e sayaam ast imrooz

The month of fasting has come to an end
Let's go and drink with a beautiful friend

Go, ask the sun to please not rise
On the moon of mine I'm feasting my eyes

With ladies of the night, sitting in the saloon
Even the preacher is singing a different tune

So go, and tell the nightingale
The rose is coming; it's no time to wail

And tell the censor to please calm down
On wine and women he shouldn't frown

For with all his saintly and pious pals
The sheik is chasing also the gals

And tell our HAFIZ to please come along
With wine and women there is nothing wrong

153

Saba ba muqdam e gul raah e rooh bakhshad baaz

The breeze and flowers are a comfort to soul
Go, tell the birds to trill and troll

O heart of mine, please don't cry
You can't have life without low and high

And look at me; although I am old
On me the beauties still have a hold

Tell not your rival about your pain
He can't be trusted; he's worthless and vain

And trust not either her scented hair
Don't count on fragrance; it goes everywhere

And trusting her face I would neither advise
For it is the focus of a million eyes

And if she hurts you, O heart of mine
You must forbear; you must resign

If proud is your rival, you should let him be
But, HAFIZ, don't give up your humility

154

Munam keh deeda ba deedaar e dost kardam baaz

At last my gal I was able to see
By the grace of God it came to be

Gentle and meek a lover must be
Give up he can't his humility

You can't have joys without the tears
Love is a mixture of hopes and fears

In the temple of love you offer your blood
Not an ounce or two but a virtual flood

The way of a mystic is full of woes
It has ups and downs, and highs and lows

In the game of love the stakes are high
And without the wine you can't get by

On the wings of wishes you mustn't fly
On the beautiful women you cannot rely

My praise and worship her charm is above
Her grace and beauty don't need my love

But, HAFIZ, when you recite your verse
They love it all over the universe

155

Hazaar shukr keh deedam ba kaam e khaishat baaz

Thank God at last she has come around
In me a lover she has finally found

The way of a mystic is full of woes
With ups, and downs, and highs, and lows

It's best to hide from your rival the pain
For he is so haughty, so worthless, so vain

Oh, when mascara she puts on her lashes
She stabs my chest: my heart she slashes

And when at night she comes to saloon
Her radiance makes it look like noon

In love there're joys, and hopes, and fears
With an occasional laugh and a lot of tears

But she's so lovely, so tall, so slim
And keeps her hair in such a trim

So when she gives me sorrow and pain
All night I sob and cry in vain

But, HAFIZ, when I do hear you recite
I feel that this world is quite all right

156

O breeze, when you go to her lovely vale
The dirt on the ground with a kiss you hail

And go if you where she happens to live
Greetings a million to her you give

Then kiss her feet and beg her to come
For soon to the pain I'm going to succumb

And bring some wine and let me drink
And tell not the censor and neither his fink

I'll lay my life for her charming eyes
And if I'm a fool, I don't apologize

And although I have to pay the price
Never will I take the preacher's advice

I know, to my rival she is always sweet
And I'm the one who takes all the heat

In the game of love the stakes are high
But I don't care; I'm willing to die

And believe me, HAFIZ, it'll all be fine
If once in a while she'll drop me a line

157

Jaanaan tura keh guft kek ahwaal e ma mapurse

Who told you, my love, to ignore your lover
And his selfish rival over him to prefer?

Knows not my rival the sorrow and pain
Just hurt him a little and he will complain

You are so noble, so sweet, so kind
A way to forgive me you can always find

The secret of love if you want to know
Ask not the flame; to the moth you go

Love and devotion are beyond the preacher
And he's so fake, he can't be a teacher

Yearning and passion know not the wise
For above their logic they cannot rise

Sincere and earnest a sheik can't be
And he can see no good in a fool like me

For know I little about wealth and power
But ask me about the bird and the flower

And HAFIZ says you do not philosophize
When the spring is here, you just socialize

158

Daaram az zulf e siyaahat gila chandaan keh mapurse

A problem I have with her curly hair
My heart from it I just can't tear

I've lost my heart, my soul, my creed
And feel I so sorry for myself indeed

I know not why they don't like the wine?
It hurts no one: it's so very benign

The trouble begins with her lovely eyes
Enchant they us all and mesmerize

But the preacher always maligns the wine
It makes no sense; it's so asinine

So let's talk, HAFIZ, about the girls
And tell us about their long, long curls

159
Gulizaaray zay gulistaan e jahaan ma ra bus

In the garden there's no flower like her
And like her elegant is no conifer

Like preacher of ours there is no hypocrite
With vagrants and topers I would rather sit

In the pursuit of passion a lot is lost
And the lure of lust has a hidden cost

Oh, I am in Heaven when she is with me
Better than her company no pleasure can be

Living in her street I find very nice
I would rather be there than in paradise

For the wealth and power I do not conspire
Being close to my love is all I desire

With her sometimes when I am alone
Both heaven and earth I feel I own

Except for my gal I don't want a thing
I'm only a pauper; I'm not a king

This quest of Heaven I find bizarre
I'm nothing but a toper; take me to the bar

By the flowing water when I sit and drink
Of our passing nature I can only think

With your gift of rhyming and the poetic strain
If I were you, HAFIZ, I would not complain

160

Ager rafeeq e shafeeqi darustpaimaan baash

Your pledge to your lover you shouldn't forget
Your company you owe him, and it is a debt

Oh, let not your hair fly in the air
Because for your lover it becomes a snare

If you want to find the life spring
The pleasure of life you first should fling

The meaning of love a flower doesn't know
You ask the bluebird, for it has the woe

If I call you my gal, you I will demean
For you are my goddess; you are my queen

My heart should be sacred to you, my pet
Don't ever break it, for you will regret

And do be careful; it's not a game
For I'm the moth, and you're the flame

Though you are a beauty; you cannot deny
That beauty also lies in your lover's eye

And no matter how much you give him pain
Your HAFIZ, you know, will never complain

161

Baaz aa o dil e tang e mara moonis e jaan baash

Come back, come back to my lonely heart
Stay with it always, and don't ever depart

They tell me that you were asking for me
You just have to say it and there I'll be

Oh, how I love your juicy red lips
When sees them my heart, oh, how it flips

That you will be cross, oh, how it fears
So the message of love it sends with tears

Go tell the preacher to have some wine
For it will give him the knowledge divine

O mystic, go and pawn your gown
Become a toper and achieve renown

Of the wine of love have a cup or two
And if it's Ramadan, take more than a few

And if HAFIZ wants the magic bowl
In the service of Jum he should enroll

162

Baaghbaan ger punj roosay sohbat e gul baayadash

For the company of the rose if you have a desire
The patience of nightingale you better acquire

If you love her hair, you'll be in a snare
And a lot of sorrow you'll then have to bear

But anyone who looks at her beautiful face
Her love from his heart he can never erase

For the lure of her eyes you should find a cure
For a lot of misery you'll otherwise endure

From wisdom and prudence if you want to be free
You should become a toper and be just like me

To the worldly wisdom you should say good-bye
On God a mystic must always rely

From drinking wine you should never shrink
So go to the bar and drink and drink

And though a pauper, our HAFIZ thinks
Without the music you shouldn't have drinks

163
Baburd az mun qaraar o taaqat o housh

Oh, how she took my peace, my reason
The one so heartless, so full of treason

She is so wanton, so vain, so saucy
So grand, so high, so proud, so bossy

I feel in my soul a burning desire
Oh, how she has set my heart on fire

And although now I'm weak and old
On me she still has an awesome hold

My faith they plunder again and again
Her graceful neck, her beautiful chin

Those juicy lips; those charming eyes
Without them her HAFIZ cries and cries

164
Ba dour e laala qadeh geer o bairiya meebaash

The spring is here; let's drink some wine
Let's enjoy the breeze, on the lawn recline

I don't mean to say, you drink all the time
But drinking in springtime is not a crime

And if our abbot offers you some wine
You should thank God, and do not decline

To see the future in the magic bowl
In the service of Jum you should first enroll

The problems of the world if you want to solve
In the affairs of life you should yourself involve

But the saying of the mystics you cannot neglect
And loyalty from the world you shouldn't expect

So, HAFIZ, you should also become like me
In the company of topers you should try to be

165

Chun barshakist saba zulf e ambarafshaanash

When the breeze does bring the scent of her hair
It brings to life the lovers everywhere

Is there a friend to whom I can show
The pain of her parting, and hope he'd know?

My message of love I send with the breeze
And beg it to go and give it to her please

But tell her when I that she's like a rose
To making her cross I come very close

The nature of love you can't comprehend
For it has no beginning; it has no end

Its inner sanctum you cannot reach
It defies description; it's beyond speech

In no one its secrets can you confide
For it is like fragrance, you can never hide

And when it falls in it, no matter how clever
Come out of it your heart can never

But, HAFIZ, in the garden the nightingale
To sing your verses it never does fail

166

Chun jaam e laal e to nosham kuja bamaanad hoash

When I kiss your lips I lose my head
And with a look from you I feel I'm dead

O free me not and say farewell
Or me to the keeper of the bar you sell

For him I'll fetch and carry the wine
And service and drinking I'll there combine

When I sing like a bird, my song is a hit
I can't keep quiet; I'm not going to quit

When I'm without you I lose my peace
In talking about you though I find release

Drinking, O censor, please don't forbid
I'm a great lover; I'm not just a kid

For when your darling offers you the wine
In Heaven and Earth there's nothing so divine

And, HAFIZ, I'm a lover and not a nit wit
Don't tell me to be quiet, don't ask me to quit

167

Dar ahd e baadshaah e khatabakhsh o jurmpoash

In the reign of our king so generous, so kind
The sheik and the preacher in the bar we find

The censor now carries a bottle of wine
And the mystic has also left the shrine

To the keeper of the bar when I talked about sheik
And said that to me he looks rather fake

He looked at me and said with a smile
That damning such people was not our style

So since it was spring and the weather was fine
I begged the barmaid to get me some wine

Telling her that being so poor, so meek
Because I'm a lover, indulgence I seek

Our king is so brave, so noble, so kind
That a ruler like him is difficult to find

Him, for his wisdom, we all applaud
And he also enjoys the favor of God

I thank my Maker again and again
I am so lucky, I cannot complain

And last night, HAFIZ, I heard a voice
Which said I should drink, and dance, and rejoice

168
Dilam rameeda shud o ghaafilam mun e durwaish

She took my heart, I didn't even know
But then I'm a man who can't say no

The preacher tells me I'll go to hell
For I gave my heart to an infidel

Oh, how I love her long eyelashes
With them my heart oh, how she slashes

But no matter how much she gives me pain
I am her slave; I just can't complain

My heart to examine when the doctor proceeds
From every little wound it bleeds and bleeds

My heart is a drop but thinks it's an ocean
From where, God knows, it got this notion?

But whether it was Caesar or Alexander
They went into dust with all their splendor

I know not why they think it's funny
When I go to the bar and have no money?

And don't think, HAFIZ, she's your honey
For you cannot have her without the money

169

Doash baa mun guft pinhaan raazdaanay taizhoash

To me said a wise man, "Would it not be nice
From the tavern keeper if you took advice

"If you take it easy, you wouldn't have to sweat
For the harder you push, the tougher it'll get"

He then gave me a cup full of wine
And said, "If you drank it, you'll feel fine"

He said, "After drinking, you shouldn't feel odd
At night if you hear from the angel of God

"Your inner feelings you shouldn't betray
When you are a lover, you've nothing to say

"And if nothing very wise there is to say
Your lack of wisdom you shouldn't display

"Even if it's painful, you should always smile
For you are a lover and not a juvenile

"And if you are foolish, you'll pay the price
So listen to the wise, and take their advice

"And, HAFIZ, drink as much as you can find
Our king understands; he is noble and kind"

170

Sahar zay haatif e ghaibam raseed muzhda ba goash

Last night an angel gave me the news
It's Shuja's reign; you can freely booze

Gone are the days when the folks were afraid
What they wanted to say, they would usually evade

The things and knowledge they would never betray
They can now come out and very boldly say

For the fear of censor they would drink at home
But now with the gals they drink and roam

Those, in his presence, who used to quake
Now drunk, on their shoulders, they carry the sheik

So I keep now telling this heart of mine
"Don't be a hypocrite, let's have some wine"

So learned and liberal is our noble king
That him we worship; to his feet we cling

It's always right whatever he says
He merits our love; he deserves our praise

And, HAFIZ, our king, he knows what's right
So let's go and drink, and let's get tight

171

Soofi gulay bacheen o muraqqa ba khaar bakhsh

Look at the rose and ignore the thorn
And drinking, O preacher, do not scorn

Go sing and dance and leave the shrine
And sell your rosary for a cup of wine

And for your piety the girls don't care
So when you see them, your love you declare

And though it kills me again and again
I'm dying to kiss her dimpled chin

Drinking I cannot resist in the spring
When sitting by the water and hearing her sing

All kinds of drinks you have in your shop
O maid of the bar, just give me a drop

The evil spirits may you always defy
May God protect you from the evil eye

And drinking with the king has made me bold
Now, HAFIZ, I want wine in a cup of gold

172

Kinaar e aab o pa e baid o tab e shair o yaar e khush

A beauty singing, by the water a song
And offering wine; that's where I belong

And my lady luck, when she is with me
My life is happy as happy can be

My gems of thought when I put in my verse
I can lure the queen of the universe

At night when she comes and sits by my side
My joy and bliss I simply cannot hide

And when she drinks, her charming eyes
They allure, they enchant, they mesmerize

So like me, if you've a beautiful gal
Dwell in bliss forever you shall

And, HAFIZ, if you do not go the bar
With the beautiful girls you won't go very far

173

Ma aazmoodaaem dar ein shehr bakht e khaish

Oh, in this town we're getting nowhere
So let us get out of this nightmare

Let's go to a city where beauties are fair
For in this town there's too much despair

While taking a walk in a beautiful vale
I heard one morning a nightingale

He said that the flowers have also their woes
Their bloom doesn't last; it comes and then goes

And no matter how much he suffers from pain
A lover must bear it; he must never complain

And if he wants to have no sorrow or pain
From hurting people he should refrain

And if we could, HAFIZ, get whatever we desire
The great Jumsheed wouldn't have lost his empire

174
Mara kaareest mishkil baa dil e khaish

It's a lot of trouble, this heart of mine
And so very foolish and so asinine

When it thinks of her it cries and cries
Its pain and sorrow it cannot disguise

And when she comes, she's always in a hurry
What happens to my heart, she does not worry

And the heart of mine, when she leaves it behind
It goes looking for her but never can find

And whenever it tries, it goes astray
My heart can never find its way

And whenever it goes and looks for romance
It's always unlucky and misses the chance

But one day, HAFIZ, she'll come, I trust
And step on my heart when it is in the dust

175

Mun kharaabam zay gham e yaar e kharaabaati e khaish

Her every glance is so like a dart
Oh, how it wounds my woeful heart

Ever since with love that I've been blessed
In everything else I have lost interest

But the blessing is not without its cost
Without her help I'm completely lost

For among the beauties she wears the crown
Her hair is dark; her skin is brown

When she looks at you, her brown eyes
They charm, they enchant, they mesmerize

And her curly hair when it flies in the air
Even the devout Muslims don't have a prayer

Your heart, from loving her, you cannot desist
It's no use trying; it just can't resist

So for her favor if you yearn and crave
Surrender your will, and become her slave

But, HAFIZ, beware of her deadly dart
It never has missed a lover's heart

176

Hatifay az goasha e maikhaana doash

Last night an angel said with a wink
You go to the bar and dance and drink

Our Lord is forgiving, loving, and kind
A little bit of sinning He does not mind

The mercy of God is beyond any bound
His wisdom and knowledge are very profound

Though fate is something you can't modify
To get what you want you should always try

Your heart is above and beyond your reason
So drink and dance and have some fun

Go, sit with your gal and play with her hair
And leave the rest in the barman's care

Our Shuja, the king, is pious and wise
His prudence and wisdom even angels recognize

His virtue and goodness you cannot deny
May God protect him from the evil eye

To HAFIZ he's always very generous and kind
A king like him you just cannot find

177

Bia keh meeshunawam boo e jaan az aan aariz

My soul is scented by her rosy cheek
And without its glow my life is bleak

Walking in the garden she shames the flowers
And seeing her stature, the conifer cowers

On earth her beauty has so much fame
That the houris in Heaven are put to shame

Her golden curls, when they fly in the air
The musk is humbled by the scent of her hair

Seeing her whiteness the lily has woes
Her cheek is redder than the reddest rose

Her beauty shames at night the moon
Her face is brighter than the sun at noon

But, HAFIZ, your verses whenever she hears
Them she admires; them she reveres

178

Husn o jamaal e to jahaan jumla garift tool o arz

Your glow has humbled the glorious moon
To your charm, my love, no one is immune

From your radiance the sun gets the light
Your beauty has conquered the world outright

Everybody yearns to see your face
The kings pay homage to your charm and grace

There isn't a man your lips can't lure
And there is no ill your kiss can't cure

And for HAFIZ also it's a great treat
If once in a while he can kiss your feet

179
Zay chashm e bad rukh e khoob e tura Khuda haafiz

She's so bashful, so lovely, so shy
May God protect her from the evil eye

And though with a look she can devastate
With a kiss, when she likes, she'll compensate

From loving her though it's best to abstain
If you want to avoid much sorrow and pain

And even if you suffer, you never should fight
Because her wrath you will surely invite

Your union with her shall never occur
No matter how much you yearn for her

Your love for her will take its toll
Though trying to have her is a worthy goal

So let's go to HAFIZ and hear him sing
Because of the poets he is the king

180
Sahar chu bulbul e baidil damay shudam dar baagh

I went to the garden and drank some ale
And heard the wailing of the nightingale

Blooming there also was a beautiful rose
But, unlike the birds, it had no woes

It looked so happy, so vigorous, so proud
Standing alone and above the crowd

The narcissus also was looking very grand
Had a tulip in waiting with a cup in hand

The iris there also was lashing its tongue
Scolding them all, whether old or young

And holding a flask was there a lass
Pouring red wine in everyone's glass

And there was HAFIZ singing his song
And telling us to come and sing along

181

Zabaan e khaama nadaarad sar e bayaan e firaaq

If the pain of parting I could only explain
I would have told you why I'm insane

It is not that I do not have any endurance
Or that I've lost my control or assurance

It has been ages since I saw her last
Oh, how can I forget our glorious past?

There was a time when I stood very high
But now I have become a very humble guy

With her when I flew, my limit was the sky
Now I've lost my wings, I can hardly fly

So now in her absence I cry and cry
And feel as if I am about to die

I have lost all hopes, I'm completely lost
It seems my patience I'm going to exhaust

I cannot sail; I have lost my form
My boat of patience is facing a storm

But I love her still with my heart and soul
And one day to have her is still my goal

This pain of parting may God destroy
My life is very sad; it has no joy

It is totally on fire, this heart of mine
In the cup is my blood instead of the wine

Despite it, HAFIZ, my love is my guide
And the pain of parting I take in stride

182

Mabaad kas chu mun e khasta mubtala e firaaq

The pain of parting may you never endure
May you never experience a siren's allure

A beggar I am; my love is profane
And I have endured a lot of pain

Being wretched and lonely I do not enjoy
Oh, how this pain I would like to destroy

But where should I go and what should I do?
I'm completely lost; I have no clue

My life is sad; there is no joy
This pain of mine may God destroy

If the pain of parting could feel my pain
It won't endure it; it would go insane

I have no hope; there is only despair
This pain, O God, was I born to bear?

So, HAFIZ, I feel like a nightingale
Having lost his rose, who can only wail

183

Muqaam e amn o mai e baighash o rafeeq e shafeeq

A nice place, a kind friend, and the vintage wine
Something like this you just cannot decline

The secret of joy is in having a friend
And a friend on whom you can really depend

If you want to find God, give up your pride
And make your love for Him your guide

Our pleasures are empty and the world is naught
It's all a dream and a figment of thought

Enjoy what you have and don't ask for more
Because on your way there're robbers galore

The maid of the bar, she is truly divine
Just see how she wets her lips with the wine

If you do not kiss it, it would be sin
For nothing is sweeter than her dimpled chin

Just see how she serves and how she smiles
Our faith and reason, oh, how she beguiles

And look at her body and her narrow waist
For whoever made her had a wonderful taste

And see how her lips are always so red
Like the tears her lovers are prone to shed

And, HAFIZ, when she tells you that she's your slave
You are easily fooled and you rave and rave

184

Hazaar dushmanam ar meekunand qasd e halaak

Me my rivals if they try to harm
Them, with your help, I can easily disarm

What keeps me alive is my stubborn hope
Without it otherwise I just cannot cope

If the scent of your hair brings not the air
I'll simply go mad; I'll tear out my hair

When I think of you, I can't go to sleep
Without you quiet I just cannot keep

If you gave me poison, I'll readily take
But help from my rivals I'll simply forsake

Only a lover knows the worth of his girl
For only a jeweler can tell the price of a pearl

You are my predator and I'll say hurray
Whenever you come and make me your prey

And HAFIZ knows, when I go to your street
I feel honored if I can kiss your feet

185

Ager ba koo e to baashad mara majaal e wasool

If only they would let me be in her street
She just might see me, and we might meet

Her curls have robbed me of my peace of mind
Her eyes have made my love so blind

My heart has become so clean and pure
And there's no ill that my love can't cure

And now if they hang me or crucify
I'll live forever, for the lovers don't die

I'll always have hope; I will not despair
Even when she rejects my every prayer

I have no money; I possess no power
I cannot approach her; she lives in a tower

Oh, where should I go and what should I do
But whatever I do, she won't say boo

My heart is mad;: it's totally insane
For it should be painful even for the pain

But to you, O HAFIZ, I cannot complain
For the wise can't feel a lover's pain

186

Aey rukhat chu khuld o laalat salsabeel

Her mouth is the spring of paradise
The tired and the thirsty it does entice

Her ruby lips, which guard the spring
Much milk and honey to it they bring

Her every look is much like a dart
It jabs, it stabs, it wounds the heart

The fire of love that's burning in my soul
It has consumed my heart; it's out of control

In beauty and grace, she is like a flower
I cannot have her; it's beyond my power

But talking about my verses, I'm not shy
Their beauty and charm no one can deny

Everyone, who hears them, does applaud
And thinks that they've been revealed by God

And the verses which I write about the girls
They are as precious as the stings of pearls

But hanging from the tree, she's like a peach
I'm short and lame; she is beyond my reach

But in writing verses I'm far from tame
My words have meanings; they're not lame

Of the words though, HAFIZ, there's no dearth
If they don't have meaning, they have no worth

187
Ba ahd e gul shudam az toba e sharaab khijal

I gave up drinking but during the spring
When the flowers came, I felt the sting

A cup of wine is what I need
With the preacher's views I've never agreed

And thinking of her I cried and cried
I could not sleep; I gasped and sighed

Her lovely face is better than the moon
Its glow outshines the sun at noon

I'm under the spell of my beautiful belle
There is no more to ask and no more to tell

When she holds the cup, this gal of mine
Her ruby red lips do shame the wine

Like silk are soft her golden curls
Her teeth are whiter than the whitest pearls

But, HAFIZ, your verses are also divine
And when you recite them, you shine and shine

188

Ba sahr e chashm e to aey laabat e khajistakhisaal

By the magical eyes of my beautiful doll
By her graceful figure, so slim and tall

By the fountain of life that is in her lips
By her narrow waist and her swinging hips

By her lovely face that looks like a rose
By her glowing cheeks and her precious nose

By her silken tresses and her golden curls
By her voluptuous mouth which is full of pearls

By her playful eyes and the way she winks
By the wine red and the way she drinks

By the musk and incense of her curly hair
By the scent that surrounds her everywhere

By the fragrant dust that blows in her street
By the sacred dirt that covers her feet

By her charming manners, her elegance and grace
By her stately carriage, her poise and her pace

For her pity and kindness does HAFIZ crave
He remains her humble and a lowly slave

189

Daara e jahaan nusrat deen khusrav e kaamil

He is a ruler you can completely trust
Yahya, the king, is so learned and just

In matters of faith, in his righteous reign
His subjects have all made enormous gain

When it comes to giving, he's generous and kind
His grandeur can be seen by even the blind

He has the keenest mind and the mightiest pen
And nothing in the world is beyond his ken

Everyone in his realm about him raves
The sun and the moon are also his slaves

In the court when they see his lively stance
The stars in heaven all begin to dance

O king, be happy and drink your wine
And you'll have luck and you'll be fine

And Heaven, when it finds you fair and just
Your foes and rivals it'll surely bust

And since HAFIZ knows you're so very kind
He worries not where his bread he'll find

190
Rehrawaan ra ishq bus baashad daleel

For a mystic love is the only guide
I have given her all what I've inside

For her my tears are just not enough
She wants my blood, for that's her stuff

To live without wine I just can't bear
And I won't go to Heaven if she isn't there

With love she has set my heart on fire
And it is consuming my being entire

If afraid of storm, a ship don't board
And don't buy an elephant if you cannot afford

The journey of a mystic is a difficult ride
So you should make love your only guide

Our king, may he live in the best of health
And may God reward him with honor and wealth

He's also very handsome, and valiant, and brave
And everyone is happy to be his slave

And HAFIZ is also in love with him
For him he'll give his life and limb

191
Saaqi biyaar baada keh aamad zamaan e gul

Oh, bring out the wine; the flowers are here
For abstain I cannot at this time of the year

Let's go to the garden and have some fun
Let's sing like the birds and sit in the sun

Let's look at the colors, red, blue, and pink
By the beds of flowers let's sit and drink

Some beautiful girls let's go and find
Let's drink with them and let's unwind

But, HAFIZ, before we drink and sing
Let's thank our Maker for the flowers of spring

192

Shamato rooh widaadun shamato burqa wisaal

I don't know how to thank the air
For bringing to me the scent of her hair

Don't sing her praises, O singer please
Her beauty has taken my peace and ease

But don't you complain, O heart of mine
One day she'll come, and you'll be fine

And what if she comes and does not fight
Would it not give you a great delight?

And when she comes, I'll go out to meet
With a ton of flowers to lay at her feet

And a million kisses I'll go and shower
On her beautiful mouth that looks like a flower

But now my heart is full of pain
My grief and sorrow are hard to explain

And being a captive of her raven hair
I have been caught in a deadly snare

But to her I cannot ever complain
My pain and sorrow, she thinks, I feign

And she does hurt me, HAFIZ, at will
And me, she says, she has a right to kill

193

Her kas keh nadaarad ba jahaan mehr e to dar dil

Oh, how can people not love my girl?
For she's a flawless and a beautiful pearl

I would rather die of sorrow and woe
Than be without her and let her go

Don't fall in love, I am always told
The wise are heartless; oh, they are so cold

And though the world I've gone around
Someone like her I have never found

O preacher, please just go to the bar
And see how she stands out like a star

And ever since she has been kind to me
My rivals are puzzled; they're totally at sea

And, HAFIZ, I love the keeper of the bar
Oh, he is so wise; he is truly a star

194

Ein cheh shoareest keh dar dour e qamar meebeenam

Oh, what is happening is beyond belief
One day we'll all be coming to grief

Every day we hope that things will be better
Knowing that tomorrow only worse will occur

Here fools are fed with milk and honey
And the wise starve and have no money

The asses are loaded with gems and gold
And the steeds are given the shoulder cold

Here a daughter is ready to kill her mother
His father a son is trying to smother

There brothers are fighting with daggers and guns
And the fathers are ready to banish the sons

So listen to HAFIZ and take his advice
He always has something to say very nice

195
Barkhaiz ta rareeq e takalluf riha kunaem

The pleasures of life let's all leave behind
And the way of the mystic let's go and find

And when with others she is so very nice
Let me also try and break the ice

It's better to sin and be in a jam
Than be a preacher and a total sham

A little bit of sinning God doesn't mind
For He's so loving, so generous, so kind

I promise, next time when she comes to me
I'll never let her go, and mine she'll be

And when someday I'll ask for a kiss
A plea like this she will not dismiss

And although, HAFIZ, the life is short
As long as I live I'll be her consort

196

Ba azm e toba sahar guftam istakhaara kunam

In the winter months when I gave up drinking
Of the coming of spring I wasn't really thinking

But now that everyone is drinking scotch
I can't just sit out and merely watch

At a time like this if I did abstain
My friends will think that I'm insane

Indeed in future if I give up the booze
My drinking friends I am all going to lose

Oh, how I wish that my gal were here
And with her I'd be sitting and drinking the beer

And with a regular job since I can't go far
I think I should become the owner of a bar

And then I would sit and drink with my gal
And that won't be good for my rival's morale

At being a toper I won't then stop
I will conquer the world and be on top

And if, while drinking, she gave me a kiss
No pleasure of the world I'll ever miss

And day and night I'll dance and sing
She'll be my queen and I'll be the king

And not being a censor, or a preacher or a shrink
I won't tell the people that they shouldn't drink

His drinking then HAFIZ won't have to hide
He'll sit in the open and drink with pride

197

Bai to aey sarv e rawaan baa gul o gulshan cheh kunam

Without my cypress, it seems rather silly
My going to the garden and looking at the lily

My rival, when he stops her from coming to my place
In the mirror of my heart I can see her face

The preacher, when he scolds me, he does not know
It's the will of God; He has made me so

And what He makes, only He can break
And whatever He gives, only He can take

And when He sets a bush on fire
Our bodies and souls He illumines entire

His will even Rustam cannot defy
And a sultan can't question and ask Him why?

And when with her parting she punishes me
I have to accept it as God's decree

But, HAFIZ, this earth is not for me
I belong to Eden; it's a legacy

198

Ba roe aey tabeebam az sar keh khabar zay sar nadaaram

O doctor please, don't waste your time
Obscure is my ill, no reason, no rhyme

If you want to help, give me some wine
And let me have a cup, and I'll be fine

This ailment of mine only she can cure
Without her my pain I cannot endure

And though she's gracious and sweet as honey
I simply can't have her without any money

I do want to go and live in her street
Only there I can find a peaceful retreat

Her love from my heart I cannot part
For love her I do with all my heart

So, HAFIZ, you see I am in a bind
For a cure for me only she can find

199
Chira na dar pay e azm e dayaar e khud baasham

Since Garden of Eden is my true home
How long in this world am I going to roam?

I feel like a beggar in a foreign land
I should go home and be in command

To Heaven I should go and find a retreat
And meet my Maker and be at His feet

When the purpose of life is so obscure
This pain of parting I shouldn't endure

I shouldn't complain and condemn my fate
Only I am to blame for my sorry state

Nothing have I done but thirst and lust
I should now be good and be good I must

And, HAFIZ, it's time for me to decide
And make the will of God my only guide

200
Haasha keh mun ba mousam e gul tark e mai kunam

To give up drinking when the flowers are here
It makes no sense; it sounds rather queer

Let us give up piety and seek romance
And enjoy the music, and sing, and dance

Rather than listen to the learned and wise
Let's drink with the girls, and look in their eyes

Let's enjoy our love, and not be in a hurry
And about pain of parting let's not worry

For the life is short and the time flies
Even the king of kings can't escape demise

And if we have sinned, God doesn't mind
For He is so generous, forgiving, and kind

I have wine in my blood as I have salt
So if I want to drink, it is not my fault

But, HAFIZ, my life, though it is sweet
I now want to lay it at my Maker's feet

201

Khurram aan rooz kazein manzil e weeraan barawam

When I leave this world, I'll be happy and gay
I'll meet my Maker; with Him I'll stay

Without Him in life there is only dismay
I feel like a stranger who has lost his way

I find this world so dingy and bleak
My heart is sick, and I feel so weak

For I'm not happy in this worldly empire
In the kingdom of Solomon I'd like to retire

And when I'll see my Maker's face
With tears I'll enter the realm of grace

But before I leave, since it is not too far
I'll go, and sing, and dance in the bar

And I will be dancing and having the fun
Like a speck of dirt in the beam of the sun

And although my journey is full of woe
I'll take it easy whenever I go

And, HAFIZ, if I couldn't find my way
I'll become the Premier's protégé

202

Khayaal e roo e to ger bagzarad ba gulshan e chashm

When you, in your absence, I visualize
My heart leaps up and comes into my eyes

So come and you my heart will greet
By laying the gems and pearls at your feet

And let me see your beautiful face
And make my heart your resting place

Without you, darling, it cries and cries
Until the blood comes out of my eyes

The very first time when my heart saw you
It became your prey, and nothing it could do

In the hope that come per chance you might
It sits and waits for you all night

So HAFIZ says, you should be good to my heart
And kill it not with your eye's dart

203

Dar kharaabaat e mughaan noor e Khuda meebeenam

I see in the tavern the glory of God
But everyone thinks it's all very odd

Wherever I look I see His face
His charm, His beauty, His glory, His grace

No scent, no incense, no musk can match
The scent of His being that He can dispatch

His kingdom is vast; His realm is grand
And nothing can move without His command

A lover, a toper, whatever I am
He is my shepherd and I am His lamb

Being not with Him I cannot bear
His scent and fragrance when I smell everywhere

I moan, I groan, I sob, and I sigh
But I'm also happy and I don't know why?

And whoever drinks the wine of love
Among angels and men He stands above

O preacher don't brag about the House of God
For I have seen Him, so I'm not awed

And HAFIZ, although he may be odd
He is a lover who's in love with God

204

Doash soda e rukhash guftam zay sar bairoon kunam

When I said I was crazy about her not
She said I was maddest of the crazy lot

When I said she was slim like a cypress tree
She was very offended and didn't agree

So being a man who cannot tell lies
I simply decided to apologize

O maid of the bar, do get me some ale
My love has made me so weak and pale

But if someday I could get my gal
The richest of the rich become I shall

So go and tell my love, O breeze
That I do beg her to come back please

And that HAFIZ knows I pray and pray
For her beauty and health all night, all day

205
Dar nihaankhaana e ishrat sanamay khush daaram

I'm in love with a beautiful girl
In her I have found a precious pearl

Whenever she comes to my humble place
I offer her wine and a warm embrace

But when I play and mess up her hair
She wants to split and go elsewhere

A toper, a beggar, a tramp I am
But being a lover, I don't give a damn

Her face is like a beautiful rose
And I'm so pale with all my woes

Her gaze is like a deadly dart
It jabs, it stabs, it wounds my heart

And although our bonds are beautiful
Between us there's also some push and pull

So love has, HAFIZ, both joy and pain
But then this is life, and I can't complain

206
Deeshab ba sayl e ashk reh e khaab meezadam

Last night all night I could not sleep
I thought of her face and began to weep

And then when I thought of her lips maroon
I felt like kissing the face of the moon

And when I remembered her bow-like brow
I was hit by an arrow and could only say - ow!

But then I decided to go to the bar
And listen to the singer and to his guitar

But wherever I looked I saw her face
Her image from my mind I couldn't erase

And though I had fun, and played with the girls
I couldn't help thinking of her raven curls

So then my verses I started to sing
And everyone in the pub began to swing

And though, HAFIZ, there's no one who comprehends
I'm lucky to have some very nice friends

207

Deedaar shud mayessar o boas o kinaar hum

She has finally come to rest in my arms
Oh, how I love and adore her charms

I'll drink my wine and play with her hair
Of my lovely girl I'll take good care

In drinking and dancing there's nothing wrong
We'll go to the bar and sing our song

And need we do not anyone's permission
For the wine is ample; there's no prohibition

So drinking, and dancing, and singing are on
And there're no cops, and the censor is gone

So sit and relax and don't be in a hurry
Have something to drink and do not worry

And to honor the topers who're not around
Take a little bit of wine and throw it on the ground

And go to the garden and there repose
And see her beauty in the tulip and rose

The moon and the sun are slaves of hers
For she is the queen of the universe

And though to her lovers she is very cruel
Our Premier is just; he is like a jewel

The stars are nothing in comparison
He shines in glory like the morning sun

The whole world knows he is fair and just
There's no one in the world that's more august

So months and years till time does bring
And till there's autumn in the world and spring

May he command every lord and knight
And the lovely girls give him every delight

And may he have tons of gems and pearls
And be always surrounded by beautiful girls

For since the moment of his noble birth
He has controlled the heaven and earth

And since the opposites are in everything
I'm old as winter and he is young as spring

And everyone, with his kindness, he does amaze
Including HAFIZ who always sings his praise

208

Roozgaaray shud keh dar maikhaana khidmat meekunam

For years in the bar I've done my thing
And, being a tramp, I've felt like a king

A pretty little girl I'm trying to bait
And having built a trap, I sit and wait

And although I always try to be discreet
I somehow end up wandering in her street

And since she's a flirt and her lock a snare
I keep telling my heart - beware, beware!

Our preacher alas is a hypocrite
He's always threatening, and doesn't quit

But I'm not also very genuine
And only God knows how much I sin

And though my moral fabric is frayed
I believe in His mercy and I'm not afraid

And Gabriel in Heaven always says amen
A prayer for the king when I say or pen

And a plea for money whenever I bring
I'm amply rewarded by my generous king

But since I know I'm not worth a dime
I don't like to bother him all the time

And though I'm a toper but act like a sheik
Hafiz, please don't think that I am a fake

229

209
Sanama baa gham e ishq e to cheh tadbeer kunam

With my pangs of love what do I do?
All night I sit and do boohoo

For my crazy heart there is no cure
I'd like to tie it with her hair for sure

O what I go through when she is away
In writing I surely cannot convey

And why am I crazy about her hair?
Just go and see her when it flies in the air

A toper am I who loves his wine
And the beautiful girls, for they're divine

And if I cannot see my sweetie pie
I look at her picture that's in my eye

Oh, me only once if she could come and meet
I would lay my heart and soul at her feet

And if the preacher calls my love a craze
It's nothing to me whatever he says

And nothing my pain can alleviate
For, HAFIZ, it's destiny; it's my fate

210
Ishqbaazi o jawaani o sharaab e laalfaam

There're youth, and love, and ruby wine
With friends and lovers let's drink and dine

The music is lovely and the barmaid sweet
There're cordial companions with trust complete

The girls are gorgeous with eternal youth
More radiant and glorious than the moon in truth

There're golden cups with vintage wine
Touching red, red lips of the darlings divine

The neighborhood bar is jolly and nice
And the garden is blissful like paradise

The attendants are gracious and the waitresses sweet
The friends are caring and the companions discreet

The barmaids are coy with charming airs
And the beauties have locks with traps and snares

So come and join us and be a trouper
Or they will call you a party pooper

And come also because our HAFIZ is here
With Haji Quam who we all so revere

211
Gham e zamaana keh heetchash karaan nameebeenam

There is no end to my sorrow and pain
Some comfort from wine though I do obtain

Only love can define a man of God
And without it a sheik is only a fraud

When I've hangover, I need some wine
But of help in this town I see no sign

If I don't drink wine, I cannot think
And there's no one here who'll give me a drink

Oh, when I am crying, I can't see her face
And this for my eyes is a mighty disgrace

But ever since to me she has said good-bye
I cannot do anything but cry and cry

So the keeper of the bar is my only hope
For, without his help, I just can't cope

And the songs of HAFIZ do bring me peace
For the book of his verse is a masterpiece

212

Koo fursatay keh khidmat e peer e mughaan kunam

If you go and serve the keeper of the bar
And take his advice, you'll go very far

For many, many years I've served the pub
And for the rest of my life it'll be my hub

The censor goes breaking the casks of wine
So now I've to hide my bottle of mine

I carry my bottle hidden in the gown
And don't mind the censor, for he's a clown

And when the sheik shames me with all his taunt
I tell him - yes sir, but do what I want

And when my rival drives me up the tree
I thank God, HAFIZ, that she's still with me

213

Ger az ein manzil e ghurbat ba soo e khaana rawam

At the end of my journey, before home I go
To my favorite saloon a visit I'll owe

And from the saloon when I will depart
I'll sound very wise and look very smart

Of the mysteries of life I'll be aware
And leave the bar with great fanfare

In love I have had much sorrow and pain
But no matter what I'll never complain

My crazy heart is bound to her hair
And it from the bondage I cannot tear

Her brow indeed is a deadly bow
A victim of its darts I became long ago

But I play with the girls and drink my wine
For, HAFIZ, the vizier is a friend of mine

214
Ma wird e sahar bar dar e maikhaana nihaabaem

We should take our rosary to the saloon
And pray for our girl from noon to noon

Our Maker has given us the pangs of love
Ever since we've come to the earth from above

The fire of love that's burning in the heart
It consumes us all, whether dumb or smart

And though we're all different, we do concur
That we can't love anyone else but her

The sheik, when he gives us his hand to kiss
Oh, how her crimson lips do we miss

So now that our boats are getting so old
Of our precious pearl we should try to get hold

For even the people who are learned and smart
As soon as they see her, with their hearts they part

And unlike the preacher, since we aren't fake
The pleasures of life we don't have to forsake

And every day, HAFIZ, we love her more
And feel very rich although we are poor

215
Ma dar ein dar na pay e hushmat o jaah aamda aem

I am not looking for wealth or rank
Only a shelter on which I could bank

A lover am I and from heaven above
I've come to the world to seek my love

And since I've seen her beautiful face
I see in everything my Maker's grace

And with all this wealth of love in my heart
I'm a slave of my king from the very start

But being a sinner and a blundering clod
I seek and depend on the mercy of God

For God's forgiveness I constantly pray
And seek His protection all night, all day

I also feel, HAFIZ, being such a clown
I do not deserve my mystic's gown

216
Mara ahdeest baa jaanaan keh ta jaan dar badan daaram

Oh, as long as I live I will never retreat
And give up waiting for her in the street

And if she would come to my place to stay
I won't care a bit what the people say

She'll sit with me and pour me some wine
And like best of lovers we'll wine and dine

With a beautiful rose like her in my place
I'll want no flowers; I'll need no vase

With an angel like her, I'll also boast
That I'm not afraid of any demon or ghost

If a beauty would try to make me her prey
Like a guardian angel, she'll drive her away

And if the preacher would tell me not to drink
From telling him off she will not shrink

With my house like a garden in which to repose
I'll have no need for the tulip or rose

Like a candle my house she will irradiate
And like moon my night she'll illuminate

And since there will be no chaperone
We'll always be together, and we'll be alone

And HAFIZ as a toper I'll have no taint
Because Hasan is my teacher, and he's a saint

217
Maroe keh dar gham e hijr e to az jahaan barawaem

Without you, darling, I'm going to die
So come back at least to say good-bye

Come and console me before I die
For I will without you forever cry

Your juicy red lips oh, how I miss
So before I die, come give me a kiss

And put your lip upon my lip
And it with your mouth you tightly grip

On your help and charity I've come to lean
For I'm a beggar, and you are the queen

Oh, how much I want to be with you
So come back at least to say adieu

And in your street, please let me stay
Take pity on your HAFIZ; don't drive him away

218

Muzhda e wasl e to koo kaz sar e jaan barkhaizam

My Maker soon I am going to see
From the snare of being I'll soon be free

O please my God, do show me the way
Before I falter and go astray

For a throne or a crown I do not crave
I'll give up a kingdom to become your slave

The folks on my grave should come and sing
Some wine for me they should also bring

And if she could only hold me tight
Make me strong and young she might

And me no matter how the people treat
I'll never, never quit and leave her street

And no matter how much do people try
I'll not move out, and there will I die

And me if she ever comes to meet
HAFIZ, I'll gladly die at her feet

219
Mun tark e ishqbaazi o saaghar nameekunam

Her love in my heart and the wine in my cup
I have tried and tried but cannot give up

The houris in heaven have nothing on her
Her place over Eden I'll always prefer

Oh, loving is something you do not learn
There is something in you that makes you yearn

When I go to the bar and begin to drink
I simply can't stop; I go to the brink

And when the sheik tells me not to have wine
I tell him it's foolish; it's so asinine

But the keeper of the bar is a very wise man
I've become his pupil and a loyal fan

There're so many things that he can teach
But he doesn't use pulpit; he does not preach

But "Don't fall in love", when the preacher says
His ignorance great he simply displays

So, HAFIZ, I stick with the keeper of the bar
He's so very profound; he's truly a star

220

Mun na aan rindam keh tark e shaahid o saaghar kunam

I will not give up my women and wine
No matter how much the sheik does whine

When the dew drops wash the face of the flower
You just can't stay in your ivory tower

With the daffodil drunk and tulip taking wine
Not drinking in the garden is too asinine

And being a lover, I'm looking for the girls
And the pub, like a sea, is full of the pearls

And though I'm needy, penniless, and poor
Begging is something I very much abhor

With the treasure of love, I feel like a king
For when you're in love, you don't need a thing

I need no Eden in which to dwell
For my love I'm willing to burn in hell

But being a lover I also need wine
So give me the bottle and I will be fine

Oh, how I love my beautiful belle
And how I grieve when she says farewell

Though moon looks lovely in the dark of night
Alas, it borrows from the sun its light

And I tell the preacher that I'm not dumb
I know that tomorrow doesn't ever come

And though being a toper is not by choice
Now that I've become one, I simply rejoice

My girl is a flirt; she gives me a story
And believe it I do and I am not sorry

And whenever she pulls the bow of her brow
She strikes the heart and people say – wow!

When the preacher invites me to be his pal
I tell him I'm going to consult my gal

He knows that women are a weakness of mine
And that I'll not give up the bottle of wine

So, HAFIZ, whatever the circumstance
In springtime piety doesn't make sense

221

Herchand peer o khastadil o naatawaan shudam

Though I've become very old and weak
I bloom when I think of her rosy cheek

My Lord has been kind to me indeed
He has given me whatever I want or need

In my jug there's always plenty of wine
Which I drink and share with friends of mine

My gal has dark and beautiful eyes
They charm, they enchant, they mesmerize

She is like a flower, very gentle and frail
And I'm her loving nightingale

Before I met her, I was rude and crude
But now that I'm wise, I often brood

And I'm not old because of my years
I've been ravaged by my woes and fears

So now I consult the keeper of the bar
For he is very smart and truly a star

And now I go to the bar straight
I've become a toper, and that's my fate

And, HAFIZ, the barman sounds genuine
When he say God likes to forgive the sin

222

Aey noor e chashm e mun sukhanay hust goash kun

O drink and dance, and when you dine
With friends and lovers do share your wine

You're young and strong, but when they advise
You should listen to the old because they're wise

And love is above and beyond our reason
So if you're in love, your reason you shun

With the rosary and gown you cannot go far
To become a mystic you should go to the bar

The people in the pub you should try to befriend
Because on them you can really depend

When Satan comes to you to prod
You should try to seek the help of God

Otherwise you'll become a sad buffoon
With life as a long and sorrowful tune

O maid of the bar, you're so very divine
Be kind to me and give me some wine

And give your HAFIZ also a kiss
His humble plea please don't dismiss

223

Afsar e sultaan e gul paida shud az tarf e chaman

Rejoice O land, with the flowers of spring
Has come to us a great new king

With the flowers forming his mighty escort
Like a rose he holds in the garden his court

May God with gifts him always shower
And may He increase his pomp and power

Like Jum's his kingdom may he glorify
And may God protect him from the evil eye

With his mighty sword may he bring us peace
His fairness and justice may God increase

May his fathers' glory his sword restore
May it always be a part of the Persian lore

May the scent of his kindness, and tact, and care
Spread in the air of Iran everywhere

His people are in love with his charm and grace
And they yearn to see his handsome face

His commands there's no one who can defy
For he is the ruler of the earth and the sky

For his kingly favors I do also pine
From his golden jug O give me some wine

For HAFIZ tells me that I should drink
And that he is right I also think

224
Aey khusrav e khoobaan nazaray soo e gada kun

O queen of beauty, please look at me
I'm as wretched as I possibly can be

Your kind attention I sorely need
Of my humble prayer please take heed

When moon looks proud of its beauty and grace
You put it to shame by showing your face

When I see you in the garden taking a stroll
I totally go crazy and lose control

And when I see the rose and the nightingale
I miss you so much, I wail and wail

My dreadful condition you come and see
For God's sake, darling, take pity on me

And ignore my rival for he is a hood
And to me, your HAFIZ, O please be good

225

Aey roo e maahmanzar e to naubahaar e husn

The center of beauty is your glorious face
Your beauty spot is the focus of grace

And filled with magic are your charming eyes
Your golden lock is a trap in disguise

Compared to your face, the moon looks dim
When next to the cypress, you look more trim

And there's no beauty that has your tan
And no one can charm the way you can

A deadly snare in the hair you've got
And a powerful bait is your beauty spot

And there's no goddess like you in Greece
For you are the nature's masterpiece

When you talk, from them the honey drips
For the spring of life is in your lips

You shower flowers whenever you speak
But there's no flower like your rosy cheek

And HAFIZ also tells me that it's true
There's no one in this world that is like you

226
Aey labat aab e hayaat o aey qadat sarv e chaman

You are slim and trim like a cypress tree
Your lips give life; we all agree

Your brows look like the crescent moon
Your lips are red and the cheeks maroon

When the flowers see your lovely face
They envy its beauty, and charm, and grace

Like silk are soft your golden curls
Your teeth look like the flawless pearls

In rage when your lip with teeth you nip
You wound my heart and not your lip

A glimpse of you oh, how I seek
And how I love your rosy cheek

Says HAFIZ without you if your lover dies
You'll be responsible for his sad demise

227

Baalabuland ishwager e sarv e naaz e mun

My gal who's slim like a cypress tree
Has made short work of my piety

With all my learning, in the ripe old age
Oh, how this love did my heart rampage

And day and night when I cry and cry
Oh, how they pity me, the passersby

Under the arch of prayer when I go and bow
Oh, how I'm reminded of the arch of her brow

What happens to me, no one does care
But the maid of the bar who is so fair

All night I wait for the morning breeze
To bring her fragrance and put me at ease

And thinking of her I lose my sleep
Like a candle all night I laugh and I weep

And then to God I take my plea
In the earnest hope that He'll listen to me

My yearning for her she can't satisfy
Like the hapless Romeo I'm going to die

And though to my friends I lied and lied
This longing for her I could not hide

In her any feelings I could not induce
I've tried and tried and it's of no use

So look at me, I have nothing to say
And see how my rivals are jolly and gay

But HAFIZ tells me to go to the king
And beg him to help and do something

228
Bahaar e gul tarabangaiz gasht o tobashikan

The spring has brought us flowers and sun
Let's shun our sorrow and have some fun

O heart, be pure, and clean, and free
And be upright like a cypress tree

When the rose is touched by the morning air
It starts to bloom and look debonair

The hyacinth with rose looks like her hair
Covering her face when flying in the air

And adorned with flowers from side to side
The garden looks like a blushing bride

And the birds when singing and flying in the air
Give the coming of spring its dash and flair

And HAFIZ tells us to drink the wine
For in it there's surely something divine

229
Chu gul her dam ba booyat jaama bar tan

When she is away, her scent in the air
Makes me go crazy and I tear my hair

In the park when a flower sees her face
It goes insane with shame and disgrace

For me with my heart it is hard to part
But she finds it easy to take my heart

She believes whatever my rival says
And won't talk to me for days and days

Oh, covered with flesh it is like a bone
In her bosom soft the heart of stone

Like a candle I weep and weep all night
And with my flame I show my blight

And with every sigh when I respire
I feel as if I am breathing fire

And when with her feet she tramples my heart
It's completely crushed and falls apart

So, HAFIZ, you see I am totally beat
And my poor little heart is at her feet

230
Khuda ra kum nasheen baa khirqapooshaan

For God's sake don't go for the preacher or sheik
For they are by nature so totally fake

Under their gowns they hide their dirt
With the maid of the bar you should go and flirt

My gal makes me drunk and then goes away
Not the slightest remorse she does display

She is as biased as anyone can be
And has no patience for a mystic like me

In the preachers and sheiks I see no pity
But the keeper of the bar is kind and witty

Her ruby lips when the wine sees
It starts to bubble and loses its ease

And when it sees the preacher or sheik
The harp in the bar does cry with ache

In the bed she soundly sleeps all night
When her lovers are awake and very uptight

But about me, HAFIZ, she ought to worry
For a mystic's love is so full of fury

231
Zay dar dar aa o shabistaan e mun munawwar kun

O come to my place and make it bright
For the house of a mystic is in need of light

Oh, how I love your beautiful eyes
And how your brow I idolize

So come to my house and with your face
Like a lamp you brighten my dingy place

The bliss of your presence I dearly miss
Oh, how your lips I would like to kiss

In beauty the flowers you simply excel
And everything in the garden is under your spell

Without you, darling, the sky looks dark
And the stars and the moon have lost their spark

And in your absence, in my mystic's gown
I feel as if I am just a clown

So come to my place and make it shine
And pour in my cup some vintage wine

And from this cup do take a sip
And let it kiss your ruby lip

And if the preacher says you shouldn't drink
You tell him to go and see a shrink

So come my one, my only one
And shine and shame the moon and the sun

Or I will have to go to your street
In order to kiss the dirt of your feet

And there I'll sit all day, all night
And the verses of HAFIZ there I'll recite

232
Subhast o saaqia qadehay pur sharaab kun

O maid of the bar, do give me some wine
Our life is short; let's drink and dine

The world is fickle and the time flies
So let's get drunk, and don't apologize

The company of topers we ought to keep
And don't waste our nights in idle sleep

And from my skull when he makes a cup
With wine the potter should fill it up

For holy and pious I have never been
My cup without wine, oh, it'd be a sin

The life is short; it's like a bubble
So give me the wine and make it a double

The flowers have come and soon they'll go
At a time like this let the wine flow

For HAFIZ says also it's good to drink
About virtue and sin we should not think

233

Fateha chun aamdi bar sar e khastaay bakhaan

When she came to my grave to eulogize
Her breath of life did make me rise

And when she was done and leaving my grave
I wished I could follow her like a slave

And though she's supposed to heal the sick
She ignores me, thinking I'm a lunatic

She totally ignores my moans and groans
And the fire of love that's burning my bones

And although she knows the healing art
She feels my pulse but not my heart

Her beauty has set my heart on fire
And her eyes are fueling my burning desire

She always looks for symptom and sign
But the cause of my ill is the lack of wine

So since my pain I cannot endure
In the verses of HAFIZ I look for the cure

234
Karishmaay kun o bazaar e saaheri bashikan

No witchery excels the magic of your eyes
Your spell and charm no wizard denies

No prince, no lord, no aristocrat
Can wear it like you wear your hat

Every houri, and nymph, and siren, and fairy
Compared to you looks very ordinary

And though you're only a little doe
No lion can afford to be your foe

And the fragrance of hyacinth just can't compare
With the scent of your curly raven hair

And though you are as lovely as any jewel
Your precious little heart is stony and cruel

But when HAFIZ writes about you his verse
It's lovelier than anything in the universe

235

Gulberg ra zay sunbul e mushkeen naqaab kun

When you cover your face with your curly hair
Your lovers go crazy; their hair they tear

And when you look at them with dreamy eyes
Your lovers you enchant and mesmerize

And when to the park you go and smile
The flowers all there you charm and beguile

And when I see them flying in the air
I want to smell them and play with your hair

And me for it when you want to kill
Your wish, I wish, that you would fulfill

Being good to my rival and with me irate
You just can't help it; it's my fate

And when in your absence I feel dismay
Says HAFIZ, "Don't sulk; just go and pray"

236
Murgh e dilam taireest qudsi e arsh aashiaan

My heart is a bird of paradise
This lure of life is the devil's device

From the bowl of dust when it flies away
It'll go to Heaven and there it'll stay

Allover Heaven it's going to roam
Until on the pinnacle if finds a home

This bird is able to make you a king
If once it takes you under its wing

And it also has the mystical power
And it can take you to the Heavenly tower

In the Garden of Eden you're going to reside
If in your heart you find your guide

And although, HAFIZ, I'm just a clod
In my heart I have the love of God

237

Ya Rab aan aahoo e mushkeem ba Khutan baaz rasaan

Send back, O Lord, to me my doe
That lovely cypress to my garden bestow

Do breathe in my body Your spirit divine
And mend this wounded heart of mine

O You, who control the sun and the moon
Please tell my moon to come back soon

Do give me back my darling dove
For live I cannot without my love

I cry and cry without my girl
So send me back my precious pearl

Do tell my sparrow to not say no
And come and be with her loving crow

From place to place she should not roam
And find in the heart of her HAFIZ a home

238

Aey aaftaab aaienadaar e jamaal e to

Your face is like the shining sun
Every heart your beauty spot has won

Like a blooming flower, your gorgeous face
Has elegance, and beauty, and charm, and grace

You are rightly proud, O beauty queen
For you are everlasting and evergreen

You don't know how proud I'm going to be
If one day you came to visit me

The stars in heaven begin to croon
When they see in your brow the new moon

My heart is caught in your curly hair
Its every loop has a trap or a snare

For God's sake come back to me, my dear
For the spring has arrived, and the flowers are here

O I'm your lover; I love you a lot
And adore your dimples and your beauty spot

So do come to me, O light of my eye
See how in your absence I cry and cry

My yearning for you I cannot explain
And with all my pain I must not complain

And HAFIZ, I am not the only one
In love this happens to everyone

239
Aey paik e raastaan khaber e sarv e ma bagoo

O breeze, O breeze, don't let me wail
Tell about the rose to her nightingale

O don't you be afraid; you're my pal
Do tell me how is my beautiful gal?

My heart is a captive in her curly hair
So how is it like being caught in a snare?

And with all those loops and curls in her hair
How many hearts does she know are there?

O breeze, next time when you go to her place
Tell her that I'm dying to see her face

And whenever you pass through her street
Do bring for her lover the dirt of her feet

And if the birds in the park you hear crying
It is because they know that I am dying

And though she is a queen and I'm her slave
I wish she would smile and not be so grave

The wine has conquered the heart of the sheik
O maid of the bar, please give me a break

When the preacher tells me that I shouldn't drink
I tell him, he should go and see a shrink

The mystery of being only the mystics know
On us this knowledge only they can bestow

And if I'm bad, please don't be cross
Because in forgiveness there is no loss

And being a lover, I feel like a king
For though I'm poor, I don't need a thing

But HAFIZ says when I go to my queen
I may be drunk but my heart must be clean

240

Aey khoonbaha e naafa e cheen khaak e raah e to

It smells like musk, the dirt of your feet
With your glowing face the sun can't compete

When you look at them, your charming eyes
Everything in the garden they mesmerize

To you even the angels cannot say no
On the Day of Judgment they'll let you go

And when people see you, my beautiful miss
They can't help feeling the eternal bliss

And when someday I cannot see you
Count the stars all night I do

My friends at work I do not enjoy
I wish you would take me in your employ

You well know my rival; he is a hood
Why don't you like people who're good?

O please, my love, be kind to me
I'm willing to wait till eternity

And HAFIZ tells me not to complain
For one day I'll surely be free of pain

241

Aey qaba e paadshaahi raast bar baala e to

O the royal dress looks good on you
And the crown reflects your inner hue

The sun of triumph does shine on the field
Whenever it sees your sword and the shield

You make a beggar feel like a king
When you take him under your mighty wing

It is just and fair without a flaw
To all your subjects when you give the law

The ink of your pen bestows the light
To the world of darkness whenever you write

And the mighty sun from its heavenly seat
Comes down to earth to kiss your feet

What Caesar wanted and could not get
Is a gem out of many in your coronet

What I have in mind you can easily read
And O king, you give me whatever I need

And since you're generous, forgiving, and kind
The faults of your HAFIZ you do not mind

242

Ba jaan e peer e kharaabaat o haqq e sohbat e o

I swear by the service of the abbot of the pub
His place will always be my spiritual hub

And though I deserve not the Heavenly bliss
My Lord will forgive my being remiss

And yes, I love to drink the wine
But in it I see His image divine

So when you see me in the tavern drunk
Please don't treat me like a skunk

Last night the angel of God did come
And said in Heaven we're all welcome

So do not disdain me if I'm a bum
We're all His children, smart or dumb

I'm not by nature a pious man
But I try to be good as much as I can

And though I'm a sinner and a bumbling clod
I believe in the kindness and the mercy of God

And when he sees me in my sorry state
Says HAFIZ always that it is my fate

243

Taab e banafsha meedahad turra e mushsa e to

Your curly locks put violet to shame
But when you smile, do flowers the same

O my darling flower, your nightingale
He is your lover; don't let him wail

My friends and foes, me all they mock
Your love has made me their laughing stock

This love has turned me upside down
And even in my gown I look like a clown

From the woes of love I want a retreat
I would like to come and die at your feet

Oh, once I was a highly respected man
But now they mock me whenever they can

But still for you I yearn and crave
And remain your lover and a humble slave

For me in my love there is everything
And though I'm a tramp, I feel like a king

The treasure of love has made me rich
For you a kingdom I can easily ditch

So wherever you go and how much you roam
You'll always find in my heart a home

And he may sing or he may wail
Your HAFIZ will always be your nightingale

268

244
Gulbun e aish meedamad saaqi e gulizaar koo

The spring has come and the flowers are here
O maid of the bar - some wine, my dear

Oh, how many beauties have gone into earth
To carry these flowers and give them birth?

Without her, the lovers are in great despair
O breeze, do bring the scent of her hair

Without her also, the flowers look proud
Tell her to come and shame this crowd

The candle is also showing off its light
Let her show her face and make it contrite

Her ruby lips oh, how I miss
I would give my life for just a kiss

And, HAFIZ, though I'm a master of verse
My luck is bad and my fate even worse

245

Mara chashmayst khoonafshaan zay chashm e aan kamaanabroo

Her eyes have given me the tears of blood
And my tears have caused in the world a flood

Oh, I'm a slave of her dreamy eyes
And her brow and face I so idolize

I'm also a prey of her bow-like brow
Even the crescent moon to it does bow

When her crescent brow does shoot the dart
It rends the moon and breaks its heart

A look from her does for me suffice
And I feel as if I'm in paradise

And though with my rival she likes to be
She makes my day when she winks at me

Her brows and eyes have given her fame
The houris and fairies she can easily shame

When the preacher sees the arch of her brow
His arch of prayer he forgets somehow

And even though HAFIZ is very, very smart
He's also a prey of her deadly dart

246

Mutrib e khushnawa bagoo taaza ba taaza noo ba noo

O minstrel, sing your song anew
O maid of the bar, I need your brew

Please go and find me a beautiful girl
Someone who'll love me and kiss me too

I badly need something to drink
So fill my glass with a shot or two

My life is sad and my love is mad
Make me forget it; I'm feeling blue

My gal is adorable, and when adorned
She becomes a siren through and through

So when, O breeze, you go to my gal
Tell her what her HAFIZ has gotten into

247

Charaagh e roo e tura shamay gasht perwaana

When sees the flame your shining face
Like me, it's charmed by your beauty and grace

Though the wise think that a lover is mad
When they fall in love, they don't feel so bad

The candle light which brightens the night
When it hears you coming, it takes the flight

I'll die for you; it is certainly true
But there're millions and millions who'll die too

On your fiery cheek your beauty spot
It looks like coal that is burning hot

Oh, when I tell you how I feel
I love it when you say - it's no big deal

And whenever I see your lips divine
I can think of nothing but the ruby wine

And you with my rival whenever I see
I feel as if you are killing me

And HAFIZ knows that I love the wine
And that I've left for good the shrine

248

Aey keh baa silsila e zulf e daraaz aamdaie

A crazier lover you'll find nowhere
So tie me with the chain of your braided hair

O you can mix water on your lips with fire
You're surely a charmer and a great mystifier

With a look you can take the heart of a man
Only to break it as soon as you can

And you can be so proud when you speak
Even though your lover is humble and meek

But you can be also gentle and nice
After you have killed him once or twice

His belief and piety cannot save a guy
When you come to tempt him and to crucify

But I love you madly the way you are
Although I know it sounds rather bizarre

And even if you ask me never to drink
HAFIZ is my witness. I will not blink

249
Khunak naseem e moanber shamaama e dilkhaah

Carrying her fragrance, the morning breeze
Came to the flowers in the garden to tease

O beautiful bird, you be my guide
And lead me to where she does reside

That I'm still alive I cannot believe
For living without her is hard to conceive

I'm weak and old with a bleeding heart
All bent and twisted and falling apart

The morning breeze when it saw my plight
It came to me tearing the fabric of night

My love for her face, with the way I crave
Has come out as flowers from my barren grave

I know I upset her when I cry and cry
So, HAFIZ, I've decided to say good-bye

250
Dar e sara e mughan rufta bood o aabzada

With the bar all swept, and nice, and clean
The keeper of the bar was doing the routine

The topers were kneeling to show their respect
Although they're always so proud and erect

The shine of the wine was shaming the moon
And the maids were gracing the happy saloon

The angels from Heaven were also there
And the lovely houris were dancing everywhere

The beauties while drinking couldn't stay quiet
They were tempting and flirting and causing a riot

Then the lady luck also came down there
With all her glory, and pomp, and flair

I also went down just to say hello
To the keeper who said, "My good fellow

"You're coming from the shrine, a fine place
Looking in the tavern for the Divine grace

"But never will you reach your worthy goal
Unless you've awakened your sleeping soul

"But if you can perform this daring feat
The moon will bow and kiss your feet

"And your reason with all its pomp and pride
To be your slave it'll surely decide

"And our HAFIZ says if you stay in the pub
You'll become a member of a blessed club"

251
Doash raftam ba dar e maikada khaabaalooda

On the way to the bar, having left the shrine
My clothes and gown were stained with wine

The maid of the bar, when she came to attend
She saw my plight and said, "Dear friend

"Go wash and clean and change your gown
When you come to the bar, don't look like a clown

"You love my lips but don't lose control
Just take red wine; it's good for your soul

"O please don't think that I'm being cold
But don't act young when you're so old

"And those who love don't get upset
Even when drowning, they don't get wet

"Being clean and pure should be your goal
So drink white wine and clean your soul"

After listening to this, I said, "My dear
Come drink with me and don't be so severe"

Hearing this, HAFIZ, she became irate
Though she remained willing to accommodate

252

Sahargaahaan keh makhmoor e shabaana

Listening to the music, I drank all night
A headache in the morning only to invite

With violets, and roses, and tulips in season
I had no use for my logic and reason

You just can't go and touch rainbow
Without first destroying your pride and ego

No bait in the world will ever entice
A bird that is a bird of paradise

He is one in all and all in one
And besides him God there is none

If it's your Maker you want to meet
You must destroy your self-conceit

And take some wine when you go in a boat
If you want to stay on the sea afloat

Your love of self if you only can shun
You'll surely become the chosen one

And if you fall in love with the maid of the bar
She'll make you very happy and you'll go far

Her beautiful brows are like the bows
And deadly darts with them she throws

The secret of being since we cannot know
We should try, says HAFIZ, to go with the flow

253

Naseeb e mun chun kharaabaat karda ast Ilah

Since God has made me to be a toper
Your objection, O preacher, is totally improper

Because He has made the wine for me
On the Day of Judgment I'll go free

The scorn of the sheik doesn't bother me a bit
For everyone knows he is a hypocrite

He only dons his stately gown
To hide the fact that he is a clown

As a toper although I'm humble and poor
In my heart I feels like a great emperor

With the maid of the bar serving me wine
I have no use for the mosque or the shrine

So, HAFIZ, in the tavern I want to be
And the life of a beggar is right for me

254
Aey baad naseem e yaar daari

It seems you have been to her neighborhood
That's why, O breeze, you smell so good

But when you go and play with her hair
Be gentle and nice; you must take care

She is much more beautiful than you, O rose
And you keep your thorn always so close

And even in the park no plant or tree
Looks as elegant and lovely as she

And narcissus, though it looks like an eye
With her eye to compete it doesn't qualify

And cypress, though it is tall and slim
She is more stately and a lot more trim

So everything fades in comparison
And love is beyond and above our reason

And Hafiz says I shouldn't despair
To have my gal I'll have to forbear

255
Aey baikhabar ba koash keh sahibkhabar shavi

Your ignorance, O friend, don't try to hide
First know the way if you want to be a guide

The manners of loving you should try to learn
If the lover's title you would like to earn

This self is an illusion; get out of its hold
And you'll change yourself from lead to gold

The pleasures of life you must forsake
Yourself a lover if you want to make

With God if your love does make you one
Your slaves will become the moon and the sun

If your heart and soul you give Him outright
He will surely fill them with the Divine light

And if your pain and sorrow are hard to bear
He will certainly help you; do not despair

So pray to God that He shows you light
And you will develop a great insight

And, HAFIZ, if your Maker you want to meet
You go to the mystics and find a retreat

256
Aey paadsheh e khoobaan daad az gham e tanhaaie

O beauty queen, I am going insane
It's time you came and eased my pain

My love, your absence I cannot endure
My pangs of love only you can cure

Without you, darling, I brood and brood
Your absence is taxing my fortitude

Your youth and beauty will not remain
So an old man like me you shouldn't disdain

And tell the breeze when it plays with your hair
To please look me up; I'm a captive there

Your every command I'll gladly obey
You are my queen: I'll do what you say

And everything I have, to you I owe
I am a toper; I have shunned my ego

I also love God and seek His grace
And one day I hope to see His face

The snare of your hair I can't complain about
For the breeze will say I'm not very devout

So come, my dear, it will do you no harm
If you adorn the garden with your beauty and charm

And come and give me a little bit of wine
And in a crystal glass to make it shine

And HAFIZ tells me he can easily forecast
That my pain of parting is not going to last

257

Aey dar rukh e to paida anwaar e paadshaahi

O king, your face has the royal glow
What is wise and right, you always know

And may God bless your prudent pen
There's nothing in the world that's beyond its ken

From Solomon, the wise, you take your cue
So the evil spirits are scared of you

His grandeur and glory you also possess
And no one denies your skill and finesse

To do without soldiers you can easily afford
The world you can conquer with only a sword

And when with your mighty sword you appear
Your foes in the battle all shake with fear

The poor are never away from your mind
To them you're always so generous and kind

Allow me, O king, to have a little wine
I'm tired of the showy sheiks of the shrine

When your eagle puts on his head the crown
The birds take notice; they all calm down

In the long, long history of the humankind
A king like you is difficult to find

Your friends and rivals you thoroughly know
And you reward your friend and smite your foe

But please, O king, allow us the wine
And ask the censor to instantly resign

And we will all pray for you vigor and health
Your power and glory; your riches and wealth

As always, be kind and generous to us
Even though our faults are too obvious

We know you're brave, and fair, and just
And a king and a ruler we can completely trust

And don't forget HAFIZ; he's one of your slaves
And about you always he raves and raves

258

Aey dil aan beh keh kharaab az mai e gulgoon baashi

O heart, don't fear and indulge in wine
And soon you'll be like a diamond mine

And you will be clean and pure inside
And wherever you go, you'll there preside

But to get the crown you must have worth
For it is not a matter of genes or birth

And you can't be a lover without devotion
For love is a very sublime emotion

If your caravan left while you were sleeping
You can't get to it by wailing and weeping

And if you're caught in the snare of her hair
You won't get out; you won't have a prayer

So go to the bar and have a drink
And about your sorrow you do not think

And look at HAFIZ; he is the master of verse
And he drinks and lives on a meager purse

259

Aey dil agar az chaah e zanikhdaan badar aaie

O heart, you're caught in the dimple of her chin
Don't try to get out; you're not going to win

And do not you try to be too smart
Or like Adam from Eden you'll have to depart

From my tearful eyes she needs a shower
In order to blossom as a smiling flower

But in her absence when I'm about to die
May be she'll come just to say good-bye

And one day her lips when I'm dying to kiss
May be my plea she will not dismiss

And the spring of life when I'm trying to find
My kissing her mouth may be she won't mind

And may be at night when I'm crying and crying
I'll get what I want without even trying

And when I'm shedding my tears of blood
May be she will come to stem the flood

And HAFIZ tells me not to despair
For long this pain I won't have to bear

260

Aey keh bar maah az khat e mushkeen naqaab andaakhti

Your face with your curls looks like the moon
All covered with the clouds as in monsoon

On your glowing cheeks your flying hair
Presents a sight that is very, very rare

And among the beauties you are the queen
For when they see you, they all turn green

For you, my love, I crave and crave
And though I'm a toper, I remain your slave

Your love to me is precious and dear
A prize and a treasure that I so revere

When I think of you, I cannot sleep
Without you, darling, I weep and weep

From your rosy face when you lift your veil
The houris in Heaven look dull and pale

When catching a lover, you take good care
To chain him tightly with your braided hair

But we are also lucky to have a king
He is Yahya the great; he commands everything

His grandeur and glory are so complete
That the sun comes down to kiss his feet

The lions and tigers are afraid of his sword
To challenge his power no king can afford

Like our noble Jum, he is in full control
For he sees the future in his magic bowl

And he's like a torch with a flame so bright
That even to the blind he can show the light

And since HAFIZ now can drink the wine
He sings his praise and thinks he's divine

261

Aey keh dar kushtan e ma heetch madaara na kuni

In killing a lover she does not demur
For in preying and slaying she's no amateur

There is not a poison she hasn't tried
Oh, how many lovers in her hands have died?

And though she can always relieve their pain
In curing her lovers she sees no gain

And when her lovers shed blood in tears
She feels no pity, oh, she only cheers

But whatever she does, they do not mind
Since she can be also generous and kind

And I bet if our preacher only sees her once
He'll never again sound so very dunce

And if like HAFIZ he sees her brow
His arch of prayer he'll surely disavow

262

Aey keh dar koo e kharaabaat muqaamay daari

Anyone who makes the tavern his hub
With the noble Jum his shoulder he'll rub

And his nights and days if he spends with her
On him His blessings God will confer

Without her, O breeze, I have the blues
Of her please go and get some news

O preacher, come and have some wine
If on your pulpit you would like to shine

No, her my affection cannot demean
For everyone knows that she is the queen

If fidelity is something she does not know
And if she likes to stay cruel, let it be so

But tell her to go and take some advice
From the cruel fate that can also be nice

Oh, how I adore her beauty spot
As a bait for her snare it's so very hot

And like HAFIZ for her I pray and pray
And I'll always be her slave come what may

263

Aey keh mehjoorie e ushshaaq rawa meedaari

O why to your lover do you say adieu
And why do you keep him away from you?

So if I am thirsty, quench my thirst
And if I'm sick, I ought to be nursed

And don't please treat it as you see fit
You've taken my heart, now take care of it

And with my rival when you wine and dine
Please don't give him my share of the wine

My rival, as you know, is a honey-bee
From flower to flower he jumps with glee

But I cannot blame you for my sorry state
I know I completely deserve my fate

And if my poor heart has a lot of pain
It's all my fault; I cannot complain

And HAFIZ says also, I shouldn't mind
The beauties by nature are not very kind

264

Ein khirqa keh mun daram dar rehn e sharaab aula

To the keeper of the bar I should sell my gown
And my books of wisdom in the wine drown

In the endless struggle I have ruined my life
I should go to the bar and leave the strife

To no one can I tell the problems of mine
I should enjoy the music, and drink some wine

I should go and join the topers' club
And flirt with the lovely maids of the pub

For girls like these you can find nowhere
I should drink with them and play with their hair

This worldly wisdom is not for me
In love I have found my harmony

And HAFIZ says, when you aren't young
You should be calm and not high-strung

265

Ahmadullaho ala maadalatus sultaani

May Providence bless King Ahmad, the just
Who is also very brave and much august

He is a mighty king and a king of kings
From him all pomp and grandeur springs

In the twists and turns of his every lock
One sees the beauty of his royal stock

If the moon comes out when he is there
The glow of his face it cannot bear

And whoever sees his radiant face
Does fall in love with its beauty and grace

The kingdom of Iraq is so divine
That flows in Tigris the spiritual wine

So anyone who goes and kisses his feet
He finds in there a perfect retreat

Whether north, or south, or east, or west
To his fairness and justice all people attest

In him they put their faith and trust
And find his honor and glory robust

And though in his service I cannot enroll
He remains the master of my heart and soul

O breeze, his fragrance do go and bring
For his HAFIZ so misses his master and king

294

266

Ba chashm e mehr agar baa mun meham ra yak nazar booday

With loving kindness if she looks at me
You don't know how happy I'm going to be

When laying my life at her dainty feet
It's something I want to repeat and repeat

In the pageant of beauty if she drops her veil
There'll be no contest; she'll simply prevail

On me her kindness she might bestow
Of my pain and sorrow if she comes to know

This pain of parting oh, how I hate
And how I dislike when I've to wait

But if one day she comes to me
I'll be so happy; I'll die of glee

And, HAFIZ, your verses wouldn't be so neat
If kissing her lips didn't make you so sweet

267
Baa muddaie magooied israar e ishq o masti

Love and devotion knows not the sheik
For he is so arrogant, conceited, and fake

The lovers are poor and don't want wealth
In love the ailment is better than health

Your worldly knowledge is never complete
And you can't reach God through self-conceit

So the one you love, go kiss her feet
And there you'll find a perfect retreat

The worldly things all do perish fast
Only love is real; it is meant to last

But the love is not without its woes
Without the thorn you can't get a rose

So my mystic friend, come have some wine
And leave these sheiks in the holy shrine

The preachers and sheiks are all asinine
But the maids of the bar are simply divine

And drinking in the bar is quite an art
The topers may be drunk, but they are smart

And the bar has also a lot of girls
Who'll make you a captive of their raven curls

But don't go there in your mystic's gown
For the topers will think that you are a clown

And you can't shy away from the beautiful eyes
They charm, the enchant, they mesmerize

So love is not simple; it's never so easy
And it can be stormy as well as breezy

And HAFIZ says, "Beware of the beautiful girls
Because they have snares in their raven curls"

268

Ba jaan e o keh garam dastras ba jaan booday

Oh, if I could've only died at her feet
I would've considered my mission complete

And if I weren't caught in the snare of her hair
I would now be sitting in the Heaven somewhere

And if many, many lives I could obtain
For her I would be dying again and again

Without her so much I would not scream
If only I could see her in my dream

So if something like her I want to see
I look at a beautiful cypress tree

But then, O HAFIZ, I begin to wail
Like a wretched and lonely nightingale

269

Ba chashm karda am abroo e maahseemaay

The beauty of moon in her face I see
She is slim and trim like a cypress tree

She's also a queen who has control
On my heart, and body, and mind, and soul

My yearning and craving oh, how I hate
But I have no choice; I wait and wait

And though the chances are very remote
I can't help hoping she'll write me a note

Oh, how I wish she would come to my place
And brighten my life with her glowing face

My heart is aflame with a burning desire
I wish she would come to enjoy the fire

From the prison of life when I'm free
Please make my coffin from a cypress tree

Because my girl is tall and slim
And I'm a victim of her vagary and whim

And though she gives me a lot of pain
I'm so much in love, I cannot complain

And though my sorrow does never cease
In the verses of HAFIZ I find my peace

270
Baroo zaahid ba ummeeday keh daari

O preacher, you do what you have to do
And I'll go to the bar and have my brew

The tulip in the garden is holding the cup
Let's bring some wine and fill it up

I know you people think that I'm mad
But to me being mad is not so bad

From all your taboos I'm totally free
So stay, my dear preacher, away from me

I'll go and play with the beautiful girls
For I'm a captive of their golden curls

Only once in a year we get the spring
And before we're aware, it's on the wing

For nothing is eternal and everyone dies
The life is short and the time flies

But if what I say doesn't sound very nice
Let's go to HAFIZ and seek his advice

271

Bashnoo ein nukta keh khud ra zay gham aazaadeh kuni

From your pain and sorrow you'll be freed
Just kill your desire and destroy your greed

They'll turn your dust into a vat of wine
So enjoy your life, and drink, and dine

And while you're young and the flowers are here
Go play with the girls and do not fear

But you should also honor the mystics old
Because they're worth their weight in gold

And if you're a young and a beautiful gal
Be kind and boost your lover's morale

And if the grace of Heaven you want to secure
First clean your heart and make it pure

And thank the Lord for the Grand Vizier
Whom we all so adore, and love, and revere

And our dear HAFIZ you should also applaud
For he puts his faith and trust in God

272

Bulbul zay shaakh e sarv ba gulbaang e Pehlawi

A nightingale sitting on a cypress tree
Was asking the folks to come and see

With the aid of breeze, with its pull and push
How the fire of spring was burning the bush

The birds were singing and flying in the air
And the topers were sitting and drinking everywhere

But the worldly splendor you cannot trust
Even the glorious Jum is lying in the dust

When there's peace of mind, even a seat of stone
Is better than the thorny royal throne

You would rather be happy and be a clown
Than have the woes of a kingly crown

Your gal, like Jesus, does give you life
But then she kills you without a knife

When drinking with you, she's an immense joy
But when she is coy, she can also destroy

And when she drinks and sings the verse
She becomes the queen of the universe

And looking in your eyes when she serves the wine
HAFIZ, you should see her; she looks so divine

273
Buta baa ma guzaar ein keenadaari

O please my love, be nice to me
I'm your lover, not an enemy

Listen to me and take my advice
Everyone would love you if you were nice

So give me a drink for goodness' sake
This morning I have a terrible headache

And remove the veil from your glowing face
And shame the moon with your beauty and grace

And we, the topers, no one should malign
For God has made us to drink the wine

And please beware of our awesome ire
Because our sighs have a lot of fire

And look at HAFIZ who's a master of verse
He is always very nice and never adverse

274
Biaar baada o baazam rehaan zay ranjoorie

Bring some wine and ease my pain
This jag is driving me insane

And if you want my place to shine
Give me my gal and a flask of wine

If my gal is proud, she's justly so
Her look is an arrow and brow a bow

Her charming smile is a great device
Even the holiest preacher she can entice

Us lovers the learned who criticize
With just one look she can mesmerize

Needless to say that love is divine
And those who deny it are asinine

And love, though it may be a grind
The gal you seek you're going to find

And love, says HAFIZ, you must choose
For blessed are those who love and lose

275
Padeed aamad rasoom e bainawaaie

Fidelity you cannot find anywhere
Love and compassion are also not there

For talent the people just don't care
The able and the worthy are poor everywhere

Of learning and teaching no one is aware
And the life for the learned is a long nightmare

A man who is wise does go nowhere
But the one who's foolish is a millionaire

And if a poet writes a verse so fair
That it is unique and beyond compare

And when he reads it, people don't care
For him there's nothing left but despair

He has no choice but to grin and bear
The world to him is patently unfair

To remonstrate he does not dare
He can't complain; he must forbear

But HAFIZ of ours, who's wise and fair
He tells me always not to despair

276

Tura keh her cheh muraad ast dar jahaan daari

She who's so rich and debonair
For her poor lover why should she care?

She takes my heart and simply departs
For she's a queen; she rules the hearts

With my need of wine she doesn't agree
And she doesn't care for my drunken spree

Her raven locks on her white face
Oh, how they enhance her beauty and grace

To stab and wound her lovers' hearts
In her brow she keeps a million darts

My rival's jabs I would not mind
If only she'll become a little more kind

Oh, how I wish she would come to me
And from my sorrow she'd set me free

And whenever I talk of her luscious lip
Sugar from my mouth begins to drip

Her lovely curves and her narrow waist
Whoever made her had a terrific taste

Of her terrible temper but when I think
With dread my heart begins to sink

So me my grief when it overpowers
I go with HAFIZ and look at the flowers

277
Jaan fida e to keh hum jaani o hum jaanaani

Oh, you're my life, my heart, my soul
In you I've found my end, my goal

And in your street I've found my retreat
So me O please you do not mistreat

Giving one's life is not so easy
And my rival, you know, is weak and sleazy

Without you life is full of pain
But I'm in love; I cannot complain

To keep it a secret I've certainly tried
But love is something difficult to hide

And I've cried and cried for years and years
For to stay in bloom you need my tears

In the twists and turns of your raven hair
My heart is trapped in a deadly snare

But my heart is happy as it can be
It seems to like the captivity

So HAFIZ says I should stay in your street
Even if with your dog I have to eat

278
Chun dar jahaan e khoobi imrooz kaamgaari

No one in the world is lovelier than you
But you're most cruel; it's also true

In hurting your lovers you take such pride
Your scorn for them you cannot hide

Your cruel malice does never cease
And your restive lovers can have no peace

But your hapless lovers you couldn't disdain
If only you could feel their grief and pain

Oh, how I wish you would come to me
And from my sorrow you would set me free

For without you, darling, I cannot cope
I've lost my courage; I have no hope

My eyes have tears; my heart has fire
And as you can see, my condition is dire

I sometimes think it would be neat
Per chance in Heaven if we did meet

But now I feel very humble and weak
And I'm unhappy and my outlook bleak

But HAFIZ says this too shall pass
And I'll get out of this morass

279
Cheh booday ar dil e aan maah mehrbaan booday

If only my gal were kind to me
From my sorrow I would've been free

If an eternal life I could attain
I would die for my gal again and again

And if fate were also nice to me
I wouldn't have been in this agony

And if I could live in her neighborhood
It would have done me a lot of good

And if I did have a little more blood
My tears of blood would have caused a flood

And the garden in spring, if you could compare
With her busy street, it would look so bare

And though she is lovely and debonair
To me I wish she weren't so unfair

And if I could see her without her veil
I would be so happy I would never wail

And if it were, HAFIZ, not for my age
In love I would've been at the center-stage

280
Khush kard yaawari falakat rooz e daawaari

We all have a lot to be grateful to God
So count your blessings and don't be a clod

In the realm of love only those who serve
The royal honor they come to deserve

With the poor and the meek you should align
For raising the fallen is truly divine

But the pangs of love are not benign
So if you are sad, go drink some wine

This game of power you should ignore
For the kingly ways have troubles galore

And don't be dazzled by fame and renown
And become a mystic and reject the crown

In the spiritual life you'll find reward
When you're a servant and you serve the Lord

And in this life if you have a lot
On the Day of Judgment you'll be on the spot

So from a mystic take this advice
To the friends and foes do try to be nice

And like our HAFIZ if you are content
A lot of sorrow you're going to prevent

281

Dar hama daer e mughaan neest chu mun shaidaay

O look at me, for a cupful of wine
I've pawned the books and the gown of mine

My head is clouded; my heart is sad
Oh, my girl's sunshine I need so bad

And I've decided that never I shall
Drink the wine without my gal

And without my gal oh, how I've cried
I wish she would come and be at my side

And her for my burns I cannot blame
For I am the moth, and she's the flame

And when I shed my tears of blood
I feel I'm going to cause a flood

A girl like her is just not there
And living without her I cannot bear

With a cursory look she can hypnotize
For nobody has her enchanting eyes

In the bow of her brow she keeps her darts
Which jab and stab and wound the hearts

O breeze, next time when you go to her street
Do bring for me the dirt of her feet

And tell her the gossip that I heard last night
That truly gave me a terrible fright

Said the barman to me the rumors are rife
That HAFIZ doesn't believe in the afterlife

282

Deedam ba khaab doash keh maahay baraamday

Last night I saw her face in my dream
Like moon it made my house gleam

I was suddenly filled with mirth and glee
And thought she finally came back to me

And having found at last the life spring
For a moment I thought that I was a king

And like old days it was going to be
When note after note she wrote to me

But then in the picture came my rival
And put in danger my very survival

It was a nightmare, to say the least
For he turned out to be a cruel beast

Oh, love is a burden not easy to carry
And it's not for every Tom, Dick, and Harry

On me if her favors she would confer
I'll gladly give my life for her

And I'll also give her the soul of mine
If only she would give me a glass of wine

And I'll also consider it a favor supreme
If once in a while she would come in my dream

If not, in poetry I would like to immerse
And like great HAFIZ write the verse

283

Roozgaareest keh ma ra nigeraan meedaari

How long, how long do I have to wait?
Do please come back; it's getting too late

O please, my love, be nice to me
Or at least do show me some courtesy

In the garden the flowers are looking for you
With the nightingale wailing, and missing you too

And though it's old and should be wise
My heart is a fool; it cries and cries

And though I know it may not be proper
It's you, my love, who have made me a toper

But being a toper I've Jum in my soul
And my cup is like his magic bowl

But unlike him I don't have money
And without the money I can't get my honey

For so many things though I'm not fit
Thank God that I'm not a hypocrite

I need your kindness and your sympathy
So please, my love, don't be cross with me

I've given you my life, my heart, my soul
On my faith and reason you've full control

And so, my darling, for better or worse
Your beauty has conquered the universe

Your hands are covered with your lover's blood
And his tears of blood are causing a flood

But HAFIZ says this too shall pass
And I'll surely get out of this morass

284
Zeen khush raqam keh bar gul e rukhsaar meekashi

O when you powder and rouge your cheek
You make these roses look all so bleak

Oh, when I'm crying, I want to hide
I can't go out; I do have some pride

But when I remember your dreamy eyes
I am in the tavern before I realize

And when you're hunting and looking for a prey
I want to be your victim without delay

And when I think of the bow of your brow
I want your arrow in my heart and how!

So O my darling, my butterfly
May God protect you from the evil eye

Do come to your HAFIZ flying in the air
And let him drink and play with your hair

285
Sahar baa baad meeguftam hadees e aarzoomandi

To the breeze when I told my sorry tale
It said, "Have faith and you'll prevail

"I'm fully aware of your terrible plight
It is too painful to tell or write

"There's nothing in the world more sacred than love
But love and pain are like hand and glove

"And though your girl is proud and vain
One day her beauty is going to wane

"The pain she gives is hard to endure
But it's for her not difficult to cure

"And although she's very gorgeous and grand
The men she likes are stupid and bland

"Your poverty and need you shouldn't abhor
For God loves those who're needy and poor

"Of the pleasures of life reject the lure
And of wealth and power you can't be sure

"And if you seek, you're going to find
And pray to God, for He's very kind

"But when you're in love, you should be clear
That the beauties by nature are not sincere

"And listen to HAFIZ; he has the pearls
And his verses are loved by the beautiful girls"

286
Sahargeh rehraway dar sarzameenay

One day a mystic said to his friend
That it's hard for him to comprehend

Why the best-made wine only rarely clears
Without being in the bottle for forty years?

Even the wisdom of Solomon is of no use
If something good it doesn't produce

And our pious sheik, it's hard to believe
Has so many idols up his sleeve

It seems our souls are turning black
Only God can put us on the right track

Somehow our people are not very kind
Our pride has made us deaf and blind

And even the people who're wealthy and rich
Instead of giving, they like to snitch

And there's no mercy, love, or compassion
And the faith and trust are out of fashion

The beautiful girls are harsh and tart
In the bosom soft there's a stony heart

But let's not worry; we should go to the pub
And all this talk we should simply scrub

The cause of friendship we cannot advance
For even our prayers don't have a chance

And although he's a very learned man
Even our HAFIZ doesn't know his Quran

287
Saharam haatif e maikhaana ba doulatkhaahi

One night an angel came to the bar
And said, "As a toper you're the star

"You should find the cup of the noble Jum
And a prophet and a seer you'll become

"The secrets of Heaven you'll have in view
And the mystics will come and bow to you

"A toper does have the mystical power
Above kings and rulers which makes him tower

"He's more imposing than the kings and czars
For he sits on dirt and rules the stars

"In poverty and need he finds the worth
And becomes the ruler of heaven and earth

"When he sees a mystic going astray
He becomes his guide and shows him the way

"And the lowly bar in which he abides
With the heavenly stars it often collides

"And though he's poor and sits on a stone
It's much more august than a kingly throne

"To the fountain of life he is the guide
An honor, to the kings that has been denied

"As a lover of God he's above the glare
For the worldly pleasures he does not care

"And unlike HAFIZ, he does expect
No undue honor, regard, or respect"

288
Salaamay chu boo e khush aashnaie

Oh, how I salute and idolize
Those charming, enchanting, bewitching eyes

I also miss old friends of mine
My heart's bleeding; O give me some wine

I think I should go to the keeper of the bar
And ask for his help, for he's a star

The worldly pleasures are full of traps
In which are caught the best of our chaps

And though he says he's a man of God
In fact our sheik is a pious fraud

And a man who calls himself a friend
We find on him we cannot depend

But the biggest problem we have is greed
It's one thing in the world that we do not need

So the evil in us we should try to nix
And with those who're bad we shouldn't mix

We should try to help the poor and the meek
And the company of the mystics we ought to seek

And let us avoid the proud and the rude
And have nothing to do with the cruel and the crude

And HAFIZ says we shouldn't complain
And thank our Lord again and again

289
Seena maalamaal e dard ast aey dareegha merhamay

O please do something about my pain
I need a girl who's a little humane

Oh, how I love those Turko girls
Those dark-eyed houris with raven curls

But what do I do with my cruel fate
And how do I make it cooperate?

And when I talk to the wise men
They can't understand, it's beyond their ken

I feel I'm caught in a deadly snare
I wish I possessed the Herculean flair

But when you're in love you can't have peace
Your pain and sorrow do never cease

And if you're proud, you can't be a toper
For arrogance in the pub is highly improper

A man should be humble and dignified
But our world is full of arrogance and pride

But look at HAFIZ, he's humble and wise
And you feel so sorry whenever he cries

290
Saba to nikhat e aan zulf e mushkboo daari

The smell in the air is beyond compare
For it has the scent of your golden hair

A treasure of love in my heart I bear
So please, if you take it, take good care

And though, my love, you're so very nice
The men you like are the masters of vice

You're justly proud of your beauty and grace
For you're like a flower with a gorgeous face

And as long as your fragrance is in the air
For the musk and perfume no one does care

And not only is your beauty beyond compare
Even the slave girls of yours are lovely and fair

And because you're tall, and slim, and trim
You make the cypress in the park look grim

But when something I tell you not to do
You promptly ask me, "But who are you?"

You don't ever listen to what I say
But look at my rival; he gets his way

O give me some wine and make me drunk
And why should I worry, for it's all bunk?

And to love, says HAFIZ, you cannot learn
It is a privilege great that you must earn

291
Tufail e hasti e ishqand aadmi o paari

The girls are made to love and cherish
For without these beauties the love will perish

If a maiden's beauty you can't appreciate
You can't be considered a suitable mate

And if it's your Maker you want to meet
To him you should give your love complete

A beautiful girl is much like a flower
On her your possessions you ought to shower

And if you want to get its real sense
The feeling of love you must experience

For love can set your soul on fire
And beauty is worth the greatest empire

But love gives you also the peace and ease
And your prayers can ward off woe and disease

And you also experience a great delight
When you weep and worship in the middle of night

Her presence or absence don't worry about
For you have her in your heart without any doubt

But when you're in love you shouldn't ignore
That the journey of yours has dangers galore

For no matter what, you'll feel uptight
When she's with your rival all day, all night

325

But then you go to the nearest pub
And with the maids of the bar your shoulders you rub

But even in there you should never forget
That she's your queen, your own Juliet

So like our HAFIZ, when you sit in the saloon
You should watch her beauty in the beauty of the moon

292
Guftand khalaaiq keh toie Yusuf e saani

You've the beauty of Joseph, they always say
But to me you're prettier far and away

Your dazzling beauty has given you fame
And I too, as your lover, have made my name

You have charming eyes and a precious nose
And your mouth is like a budding rose

So if you promise to give me a kiss
A chance like this I will never miss

For a kiss of yours I'm willing to die
Although for me it's a pie in the sky

And since your gaze is like a dart
With the bow of your brow do strike my heart

O why don't you send a letter or two?
For head over heels I'm in love with you

Being ignored by you I cannot bear
So please don't tell me you do not care

You are slim and trim like a cypress tree
So please come to the park, and be with me

And like old HAFIZ, I'll never complain
And suffer in silence my sorrow and pain

293

Guzishti bar mun e ghamdeeda az raah e jafakaari

I know she is callous and insincere
But she is my life, and to me very dear

She always keeps my rival around
Although you know he's a murderous hound

But then she is also a beautiful doll
Even though she drives me up the wall

O maid of the bar, come give me a drink
For deep in trance I would like to sink

I'm at your mercy, so please feel free
And whatever you like, you do with me

294

Gashta az aatish e mai aariz e to gulwaaray

The wine has given your face a flush
Oh, how I love this beautiful blush

And the raven curls on your cheek and nose
They look like hyacinth covering a rose

When I see all this, I go for a drink
And feel sorry for those from wine who shrink

And I also understand why the birds so wail
When I cry for you like a nightingale

Your curly locks when they fly in the air
My desire for you I just cannot bear

Then I go to HAFIZ and hear him sing
And soon I begin to feel like a king

295
Makhmoor e jaam e ishqam saaqi badeh sharaabay

O I'm in love, give me some wine
And let me drown this sorrow of mine

And although I've tried, and tried, and tried
This love of mine there's no way to hide

Her gorgeous face I crave to see
But I'm totally dazzled when she looks at me

This waiting and waiting oh, how I hate
But to see her once I wait and wait

With a love like this it's hard to cope
For I yearn and yearn and hope and hope

So HAFIZ my friend, I've come to a conclusion
That love is a fancy; it's a pure illusion

296

Ma aem o gham e ishq e jawaanay o khayaalay

With the pangs of love oh, how do I cope?
I can see no light; I simply grope

The pain of her absence is always with me
With her I don't know when will I be?

O breeze, when you go and see my gal
Tell her what a shape I'm in, her pal

And if she asks you how have I been
Tell her I've become very weak and thin

And though people crave for money and power
I only yearn for my beautiful flower

I only want to go to her street
And kiss and worship the dirt of her feet

But HAFIZ thinks that I'm a buffoon
Because I am always crying for the moon

297
Naubahaareest dar aan koash keh khushdil baashi

O enjoy the flowers for they'll disappear
And when they return, you may not be here

The music is telling you to sing and dance
So take its advice and go into a trance

Well, I shouldn't be giving any advice to you
For you are so wise, and you know what to do

But these lovely flowers not pluck you must
For they've come from the girls who're lying in the dust

And the world of the mystics, before you explore
Its perils and dangers you shouldn't ignore

And a place of bliss if you want to secure
Of the pleasures of life you should avoid the lure

And HAFIZ says you should shun your conceit
If the one you love you want to meet

298

Waqt ra ghaneemat daan aan qadar keh batwaani

Go, have some fun and don't apologize
For the life is short and the time flies

And tell not the preacher what you want to do
For the man is shallow and doesn't have a clue

And do not argue nor get into a fight
Just thank the Lord and pray all night

And if your darling girl you somehow lose
Do not complain, and don't have the blues

The gorgeous girls with their long eyelashes
Oh, how they wound with jabs and slashes

But listen to the mystics and take their advice
Your worldly woes aren't worth the price

Our pious sheik does love the wine
But offer it not, for he'll surely decline

And though in private he'll wine and dine
In public he'll break your vats of wine

The beautiful girls have the hearts of stone
And even to the Premier their cruelty is known

But when these girls in the bar get drunk
No one can resist them, not even a monk

And when they walk, they sway in the breeze
For they are slim and trim like the cypress trees

And if you survive their charming eyes
The bows of their brows will cause your demise

And our HAFIZ says beware, beware!
Their every lock is a deadly snare

299
Hazaar jehd bakardam keh yaar e mun baashi

I've tried and tried to make you a friend
But to such an honor I could not ascend

I wish you would decide to come to my house
And see me howl, and grunt, and grouse

I promise to you I won't make a scene
And make you instead my cherished queen

With sorrow and pain I'll know how to cope
If only you'll give me a little bit of hope

Those crimson lips which I love so much
Someday with my mouth I would like to touch

Oh, you have no worry, no trouble, no woe
For you are a happy and a cheerful doe

So if you promise to give me a kiss
A chance like this I'll never miss

And though I'm old and not very bold
You in my arms I would love to hold

And when in the park we walk or stand
I wish you would let me hold your hand

For you I pine, I yearn, I crave
For you are my queen and I am your slave

And though as HAFIZ I'm loved in the city
I want your love; I need your pity

335

Read Free

English and Urdu translation in VERSE of the Persian odes of KHUSRO and HAFIZ
and
English translation in VERSE of the Urdu odes of GHALIB
by
Logging on to URL: www.writing.com/authors/khalmeed
Searching through Google under: Khalid Hameed Shaida

Buy Books
amazon. com and other etailers

1. Khusro, the Indian Orpheus, a hundred odes
2. Hafiz, the Voice of God, a hundred odes
3. Hafiz, Drunk with God, selected odes
4. Ghalib, the Indian Beloved, Urdu odes

Suraj, 6/A Naseeruddin Road, Islampura, Lahore, Pakistan.
Email: surajquarterly@yahoo.com

1. Dr. Khalid Hameed Shaida Number I with English and Urdu Translation of Ghalib
2. Dr. Khalid Hameed Shaida Number II with English and Urdu Translation of Hafiz
3. Khusro aur Iqbal with English and Urdu Translation of Khusro and Iqbal

Write to the translator: Khalid Hameed Shaida, MD
2208 Lakeway Drive, Friendswood, TX 77546, USA
Email: khalmeed@aol.com